“Over the last century Chr

as never before, with popul
this book Lionel Young ex
taken place but is also insistent that the task of spreading the gospel worldwide is unfinished.”

—**David W. Bebbington**
University of Stirling, Scotland

“This is now the best introduction to world Christianity for thoughtful, literate, everyday Christians—the very people who most need to understand the realities that Lionel Young describes. God has rocked the Christian world during the past several decades, upending what many took for granted about the church. It’s time we paid attention and participated humbly in the surprising work of God in the Global South.”

—**Douglas Sweeney**
Beeson Divinity School

“This is a compact, accessible primer full of essential facts about the link between world Christianity and mission. Young’s passion for the subject is evident in the relevant stories and personal anecdotes he skillfully weaves into the compelling narrative. I highly recommend this book to pastors, missionaries, and scholars with a growing interest in the fascinating trajectories of Christianity in the non-Western World.”

—**Kyama Mugambi**
Author of *A Spirit of Revitalization: Urban Pentecostalism in Kenya*

“The extraordinary transformation in the global composition and cultural flavor of Christianity that has taken place in the last half-century have attracted the attention of numerous scholars, but sadly have yet to penetrate the consciousness of the average churchgoer in the West. Lionel Young’s readable and stimulating survey will surely help to address that deficit, widening horizons and dispelling preconceptions.”

—**Brian Stanley**
University of Edinburgh

"Lionel Young has written a concise and exciting look at the dramatic changes occurring in global Christianity today, and I heartily recommend it. I envision pastors sharing this book with their congregations, explaining the crucial yet often unnoticed shifts within Christianity that are happening right outside our doorsteps."

—Dyron Daughrity
Pepperdine University

"I am delighted that Lionel Young has produced this book, which is based on his thorough knowledge of world Christianity and is written in a pleasingly accessible way. We lacked this very short introduction to the subject and now that need has been met—splendidly."

—Ian Randall
Cambridge Center for Christianity Worldwide

"Don't let the subtitle fool you. This 'very short introduction' will be shocking to the average Western Christian. It is staggering to see through these pages how Christianity has emerged and is flourishing in the Global South. This very short book casts a very long vision for Christian mission in the twenty-first century."

—Steve DeWitt
Author of *Eyes Wide Open: Enjoying God in Everything*

"This is an important book for anyone who cares about the state of global Christianity. Lionel Young combines his personal experience in global missions with impressive academic rigor to draw a complete picture to show how God is at work in the world in unprecedented and surprising ways."

—Rick Thompson
Global Action and Council Road Baptist Church

"This highly accessible book speaks directly to Christians in the West as the latest one-stop shop for understanding world Christianity today. Lionel Young has masterfully woven together history and the present, missions and human rights, Global North and Global South, and Catholics and Protestants to send a powerful message of Christian unity for the twenty-first century."

—Gina A. Zurlo

Center for the Study of Global Christianity,
Gordon-Conwell Theological Seminary

WORLD CHRISTIANITY and the UNFINISHED TASK

WORLD CHRISTIANITY and the UNFINISHED TASK

A Very Short Introduction

F. LIONEL YOUNG III

Foreword by
MUTHURAJ SWAMY

CASCADE *Books* • Eugene, Oregon

WORLD CHRISTIANITY AND THE UNFINISHED TASK
A Very Short Introduction

Copyright © 2021 F. Lionel Young III. All rights reserved. Except for brief quotations in critical publications or reviews, no part of this book may be reproduced in any manner without prior written permission from the publisher. Write: Permissions, Wipf and Stock Publishers, 199 W. 8th Ave., Suite 3, Eugene, OR 97401.

Cascade Books
An Imprint of Wipf and Stock Publishers
199 W. 8th Ave., Suite 3
Eugene, OR 97401

www.wipfandstock.com

PAPERBACK ISBN: 978-1-7252-6653-7
HARDCOVER ISBN: 978-1-7252-6654-4
EBOOK ISBN: 978-1-7252-6655-1

Cataloguing-in-Publication data:

Names: Young, III, F. Lionel, author. | Swamy, Muthuraj, foreword writer.

Title: World Christianity and the unfinished task : a very short introduction / F. Lionel Young III.

Description: Eugene, OR: Pickwick Publications, 2021 | Includes bibliographical references and index.

Identifiers: ISBN 978-1-7252-6653-7 (paperback) | ISBN 978-1-7252-6654-4 (hardcover) | ISBN 978-1-7252-6655-1 (ebook)

Subjects: LCSH: Missions—History | Christianity—20th century | Christianity—21st century

Classification: BR121.3 Y68 2021 (paperback) | BR121.3 (ebook)

Manufactured in the U.S.A. 06/16/21

Dedicated to my loving wife Stacy Suzann.
I will never forget our time in Africa at the foot
of the Ngong Hills. My life has never been the same.

"Pentecost, as the beginning of the new age of God's salvation,
is not a reversion to the unity of cultural uniformity;
it is an advance toward harmony in cultural diversity."

—Miroslav Volf

Contents

Foreword by Muthuraj Swamy | ix
Acknowledgments | xiii

Introduction | 1

1 Shifting Southward: How the Gospel Is Turning the World Upside Down | 11

2 Counting Every Soul on Earth: How We Know So Much about World Christianity | 32

3 Converting Colonialism: How Secular Critics of Missionaries Get It Mostly Wrong | 46

4 The Surprising Work of God: Why the Work of Western Missionaries Is Only Part of the Story | 69

5 The Unfinished Task: Why the Mission to Save the World Remains Unfinished | 88

6 The White Man's Burden: Why the West Cannot Save the Rest and Should Not Try | 101

7 A Century of Partnerships? New Trends in Missions That Could Transform the World | 120

Bibliography | 131
Index | 149

Foreword

World Christianity as a theme within the study of the history of Christianity and world missions has received significant scholarly attention during the last few decades. A vast amount of literature has been produced—and this continues—showing how this subject is central to understanding the growth of Christianity in different parts of the world. Implications are often drawn out for Christians in the West for doing world missions in the twenty-first century as Christians together. The emphasis is on learning from each other while participating in mission, rather than seeing the West as "mission giver" and the rest as "receivers."

Christianity, from the beginning, has strived to be a world movement connecting Jerusalem and the ends of the earth (Acts 1:8). We see that this begins with the mission work of the apostles in the early church who travelled to different parts of the world. This continued in medieval times, but grew rapidly during the last few centuries. Born in the context of Enlightenment and European expansion, and accompanied with a sense of urgency—"evangelizing the whole world in this generation"—modern missions took Christianity in western clothes to many parts of the world, including where Christianity already existed in localized forms.

While the efforts to make Christianity a world religion have been part of the history of Christianity for centuries, the current focus on World Christianity has emerged due to many changing factors in the twenty-first century. Primary among them is the great demographic shifts. As many studies in World Christianity have pointed out, now there are more Christians living in what is termed the Global South—Asia, Africa, Latin America, the Middle East, and Oceania—than in the Western parts of the world. This reality is very different compared to the beginning of the twentieth century, when more than 80 percent of the world's Christians still resided in the West. In the eyes of many, Christianity is no longer a Western religion, but truly a "world religion" as never before.

With this has come a critical look, among Christians, at missionary work and their histories and legacies. While not denouncing or undermining completely what Western missionaries have done in taking Christianity to different parts of the world, critical perspectives have emerged throwing new light on missionary work. With the arrival of contextual theologies and postcolonial frameworks, these approaches have been sharpened and strengthened. The missionaries' attitudes and approaches to local cultures, traditions, and histories, and their collaborations with (and distance from) colonial administrators are some important topics focused in the study of World Christianity. But, attention is increasingly paid not just to how and what missionaries contributed through their work but also to how local cultures and traditions interacted with Christianity, rather than viewing themselves as there just to be replaced by Western Christianity. Most importantly, the contextual factors surrounding the existence and growth of Christianity in the Global South—both in the past and today—often show how these are different from the Western situation and how they fuel the rapid growth of Christianity in these parts of the world. The local Christians' role in indigenous missions, ecumenical relations, and making strong connections between Christianity and the local context—all of which have not often been focused in the missionary histories and biographies—have started to receive focus in the study of World Christianity.

One of the important aspects of World Christianity, for me, is the existence of many Christianities and how they are connected. Modern Western Christianity has generally worked from the assumption of the West as *giver* of the gospel and the rest as *receiver* of this mission. But this approach has significant limitations as many historians of Christianity and missiologists have now shown. What is important in the twenty-first century is how we as Christians in different parts of the world can join hands and learn from each other in witnessing to the gospel. In the Book of Acts, Paul's missionary journeys were not always and not strictly about reaching non-Christians and planting churches. Paul spent a great deal of his time in his missionary journeys in visiting Christians and connecting them with each other (i.e., connecting Christians from different regions). The invitation to learn about World Christianity is an opportunity for Western Christians to connect with and learn from Christians living in other contexts amidst many cultures, traditions, and religions to participate in the mission of God as Christians together.

Lionel Young brings out the importance of this approach to Christian mission in this book. He invites Christians, particularly those in the West, many of whom have long neglected the story of World Christianity, to be mindful of the many Christianities that exist, particularly in the Global South. Even though there are a number of works available on World Christianity, Young's is one of the first of its kind that aims to cater to a wider audience—common Christians who want to learn about World Christianity and participate in Christian mission. He offers lucid and succinct discussions with a very simple and easy-to-follow style. Scholars and students who are looking for an up-to-date "very short introduction" to World Christianity will readily find one in this book.

As Young points out, what the theme of World Christianity reminds us is that Christian mission is an unfinished task and this is the time we move beyond the notions of "white man's burden" and the Western church as saviour of the world. In the context of many challenges affecting Christian life and practice both in the West and in the Global South, and the reality of polycentric and reverse missions, Christianity and Christian mission in the twenty-first century is more about acknowledging the many Christianities that are rooted in local cultures and contexts. It is about being connected as worldwide Christians in order to learn from each other in living and witnessing to the gospel.

Muthuraj Swamy[1]
Cambridge, Summer 2020

1. Muthuraj Swamy is the Director of the Cambridge Centre for Christianity Worldwide and a member of the Faculty of Divinity at the University of Cambridge.

Acknowledgments

I WOULD LIKE TO thank my friends at the Cambridge Centre for Christianity Worldwide (CCCW) for helping make this project possible. Muthuraj Swamy, Polly Keen, Ruth Maclean, Philip Saunders, and Ian Randall have made Cambridge feel like a home away from home and given me space for uninterrupted study and writing. I want to thank those who have read all or portions of this manuscript and offered helpful comments before publication: David Bebbington, Bailey Bada, Heath Carter, Steve DeWitt, Dyron Daughrity, Todd Johnson, Kyama Mugambi, Linda Ocholo, Ian Randall, Muthuraj Swamy, Jeff Peterson, Brian Stanley, Douglas Sweeney, Rick Thompson, and Gina Zurlo. I wish to express appreciation to Michael Thompson and Robin Parry at Cascade Books. Michael believed in this project from the beginning, and Robin provided keen editorial guidance to the end.

I am grateful for the assistance I have received from staff members at the Africa Inland Mission International archives in Nottingham, England, the Booher Library at the Seminary of the Southwest in Austin, Texas, the Cambridge University Library, the Henry C. Crowell Library at the Moody Bible Institute in Chicago, the Stitt Library at Austin Presbyterian Theological Seminary, Westcott House in Cambridge, Westminster College Library in Cambridge, and the Special Collections on Evangelism and Missions at the Billy Graham Center in Wheaton, Illinois.

I want to thank my family for their unconditional love and constant encouragement. Stacy, Fleetwood, Molly, Vesper, Robby, and Bradley are each a source of God-given joy in my life. I also want to thank my colleagues and our board members at Global Action for welcoming me so warmly into their family and encouraging me to lead, teach, study, and write for the global church and the glory of God. It is my prayer that this very short introduction will give others a better understanding of why we are all so passionate about the work we are doing together.

F. Lionel Young III
Cambridge, England

Introduction

THIS BOOK IS A very short introduction to one of the most remarkable transformations in the 2,000-year history of the church. In the year 1900 more than 80 percent of the world's Christians were either European or Anglo American—and nearly all of the world's missionaries were being sent out to Africa, Asia, or Latin America from Western nations. In an extraordinary turn of events, spanning a little more than 100 years, the demographic center of Christianity dramatically shifted to the Southern Hemisphere. Today the vast majority of Christians, nearly 70 percent, are African, Asian, or Latin American and nearly half of the world's full-time cross cultural missionaries are being sent out from the non-Western world. The secularization thesis, the notion that the world was becoming more secular, has now been overturned. Contrary to the assumptions of many people in North America and Western Europe, the world is actually becoming *more* religious. As Timothy Keller put it in a 2017 tweet, "The whole world is not getting more secular, white people are getting more secular."[1] The old maps of the religious world that still exist in the minds of many Western people are now as outdated as colonialism itself. The present work introduces readers to the phenomenal reordering of contemporary Christianity, telling the story of how it happened, and also posing the question: "Now that Christianity has grown so rapidly in the

1. Timothy Keller, Twitter post, February 6, 2017, 9:04 a.m., https://twitter.com/timkellernyc/status/828620265017974784.

non-Western world, what does this mean for the ongoing work of world mission?"[2]

The expression World Christianity (also referred to as Global Christianity) came into ascendency beginning in the 1980s as scholars began to turn their attention to the surprising growth of Christianity in Africa, Asia, and Latin America.[3] Almost without exception the available works on World Christianity have been published by academic presses for scholars and students. Dana Robert's cover article "Shifting Southward" appeared in the *International Bulletin of Missionary Research* in 2000 and marked the beginning of a new era of scholarly attention on the global church. Her work anticipated several important book-length studies on World Christianity.[4] In 2002, Philip Jenkins unveiled his award-winning work *The Next Christendom: The Coming of Global Christianity* and awakened an even larger audience to the unexpected arrival of global Christianity. As he put it most succinctly, "The era of Western Christianity has passed in our lifetimes, and the day of Southern Christianity is dawning."[5] Jenkins reprimanded Western scholars and presses for ignoring what he called "one of the transforming moments in the history of religion worldwide"—the dramatic rise of Christianity in the Global South.[6] His work moves beyond a straightforward account of the growth of non-Western Christianity and dabbles in a bit of Nostradamus-like forecasting (he admits that this is normally a taboo for historians). Jenkins

2. I recognize that British readers will prefer the word mission (singular) to the word missions (plural). For American readers, the use of the singular communicates that there is only one mission while the plural concedes that there are many different mission organizations (missions). While recognizing and appreciating this distinction, I frequently use the words interchangeably.

3. The expression World Christianity has its genesis in the ecumenical efforts of the postwar period and has been traced to the publication of Henry P. Van Dusen's 1947 work *World Christianity: Yesterday, Today, Tomorrow*. However, as Dana Robert has shown, it was not until the early 1980s that the study of World Christianity, especially its non-Western expressions, gained a wider following. See Robert, "Naming 'World Christianity,'" 1–18.

4. Robert, "Shifting Southward," 50–58.

5. Jenkins, *The Next Christendom*, 3.

6. Jenkins, *The Next Christendom*, 1.

envisions a possible "clash of civilizations" between cultures aligned with Islam and nations in Africa and Asia where Christianity is rapidly growing. His work is concerned with the possible social and political implications of global Christianity in what he calls "the next Christendom."

Douglas Jacobson's 2011 work, *The World's Christians: Who They Are, Where They Are, and How They Got There* takes a geographic-historical approach to World Christianity by surveying the global status of the four major Christian traditions. He locates the Orthodox, Catholic, Protestant, and Pentecostal/Charismatic expressions of the faith on the map of the modern world and describes how Christianity is faring in each region ("barely surviving," "thin, but alive," "hope and despair," etc.). His work provides a fairly comprehensive narrative of global Christianity along geographical and historical lines. The author's 2015 work, *Global Gospel: An Introduction to Christianity on Five Continents* is an abbreviated (and updated) version of his 2011 study. Noting the great variety that exists within the church, he picks up the language of World Christianities (plural) and argues that global variety within Christianity provides an opportunity for the followers of Christ to "learn from one another" in genuine humility.[7]

Dyron Daughrity has made significant contributions to the contemporary study of World Christianity. His 2010 work *The Changing World of Christianity: The Global History of a Borderless Religion* covers the geographic expansion of Christianity in the twentieth century while providing a comparative analysis of the Christian faith with other world religions (Muslim, Hindu, and Buddhist). He limits his discussion to those faith traditions that represent more than 1 percent of the world's population. One of Daughrity's strengths, reflected in his growing scholarly oeuvre, is his academic background in comparative religion. In his 2011 monograph, *Rising: The Amazing Story of Christianity's Resurrection in the Global South,* Daughrity offers a highly accessible discussion of important themes like the "decline of Christianity in Western Europe," the "death and resurrection Christianity in

7. Jacobson, *Global Gospel*, 230.

Russia," the status of Christianity in the United States, "African encounters with Christianity," the growth of Christianity in Asia, and "reverse mission"—the witness of non-Western Christians in Western nations. His 2015 work, *To Whom Does Christianity Belong? Critical Issues in World Christianity* takes a theological-thematic approach, exploring some of the contemporary issues raised by the diversity of the world Christian movement. These themes include theology, human sexuality, the role of women in the church, and worship/music. His latter work also serves as the introduction to a more ambitious publishing enterprise that is now producing full-length monographs by specialists on World Christianity in particular regions of the world like China,[8] Mexico,[9] India,[10] and Eastern Africa.[11]

In *World Christianity: A Historical and Theological Introduction*, Lalsangkima Pachua, a scholar from Northeast India, delves into theological themes in World Christianity and argues that "older Western Christianity" with its emphasis on the need to "rationalize" the faith for a secularized society is now in tension with the "newer Christianity of the majority world" where experiential (charismatic) Christianity is rapidly growing. In addition to his focus on theological themes, he observes that the concept of "foreign missions" is now outdated (the idea of "the West to the rest") and should be replaced with "global missions," an idea now captured in the expression, "missions from everywhere to everyone."[12] *Introducing World Christianity* (2012), edited by Charles E. Farhadian, is an ambitious collection of essays written by scholars from the global academic community covering Christianity in every region and sub-region of the world. Africa, Asia, Europe, Latin America, and North America are subdivided and treated separately (for example, the massive continent of Africa is

8. Kwong-Chan, *Understanding World Christianity: China* (2019).

9. Hartch, *Understanding World Christianity: Mexico* (2019).

10. Daughrity and Athyal, *Understanding World Christianity: India* (2016).

11. Kollman and Smedley, *Understanding World Christianity: Eastern Africa* (2015).

12. Pachau, *World Christianity*, 180–82.

broken down into four regions, while Western Europe and Eastern Europe are treated separately). The work takes an interdisciplinary approach to World Christianity by using the insights of historians, sociologists, and anthropologists who examine the impact of Christianity in contemporary society. In *Christianity as a World Religion* (2008), Sebastian and Kirsteen Kim give an encyclopedic survey of Christianity in Europe, North America, Latin America, Africa, and Asia. Their world tour also provides illuminating analyses of the varied challenges facing the church in the various regions of the world. Dana Robert's work *Christian Mission: How Christianity Became a World Religion* focuses on the history of the missionary movement and gives missionaries due credit for the rise of World Christianity. Her work does not ignore the failures and foibles of Western mission societies, though her research challenges the negative stereotypes of missionaries that abound in film and literature. Robert argues that missionaries were highly involved in humanitarian work, defenders of the rights of women and children, and that their translation work resulted in the preservation of non-Western languages and cultures. Brian Stanley's 2019 monograph *A World History of Christianity in the Twentieth Century* is written along historical-thematic lines, and surveys a wide range of topics on a global scale that illuminate contemporary issues. He tackles contemporary subjects like the response of British and American Christians to the First World War, African Christianity and decolonization, racism and genocide in the "Christian" nations of Germany and Rwanda, the relationship between Christianity, Islam, and other religions, Latin American liberation theology, and the church's continued debates on human sexuality and the ordination of women. Stanley demonstrates an impressive familiarity with the vast array of the world's geographic regions as well as the relevant peer-reviewed academic literature covering a wide geographic distribution.

The present work will be the first very short introduction for a general readership on World Christianity. I have culled from the expansive body of academic literature in the field, cutting away as much as possible, without sacrificing academic precision. My own work "stands on the shoulders of giants" and makes some of the best scholarship on World Christianity accessible for a wide readership. This book also extends the discussion beyond World Christianity to the praxis of Christian mission in the twenty-first century. It is intended to be a potted work on the subject of World Christianity, though it provides ample footnoting that will allow interested readers to deepen their understanding of the topic. It is my singular aim to "translate the message" of World Christianity and Christian mission into a short, easy-to-understand guide for the average reader. I have tried to write for the Christian layperson—*ad populum* (for the people) rather than *ad clerum* (for the clergy)—though I do hope that pastors, students, and Christian leaders will find the contents of this work edifying.

In the chapters that follow I briefly discuss the remarkable "Southern shift" of Christianity—a reality that is now well documented even though it continues to surprise many well-informed Western Christians. Chapter 1 provides a thumbnail sketch of Christianity around the world in the space of a single chapter. It briefly describes the shape and size of Christianity in each region of the world: Europe, North(ern) America, Latin America, Africa, Asia, and Oceania. The second chapter introduces readers to the fascinating people who, like the legendary "Indiana" Jones, divide their time between giving lectures in university classrooms and searching for "buried treasure" in the far-flung corners of the world. These scholars are not only recounting the work of Western missionaries who left kith and kin to toil in foreign lands, they are "counting Christians" and unearthing the buried stories of African, Asian, and Latin American Christians. The discoveries of these travel-worn academics have informed many of the ideas found throughout the work, but especially the ideas discussed in chapters 3 and 4. These chapters focus on the question of *how* Christianity actually became the most diverse religion in the world over the course of about 100 years. Researchers have learned that missionaries, in spite of the bad press they have sometimes received, were often very effective at their work. However, these now unearthed histories have also revealed that the efforts of Western missionaries were not the only (or even primary) factor contributing to the growth of the church in the non-Western world. Chapter 5 poses the question, "Now that Christianity is flourishing in the non-Western world, what does this mean for Christian mission?" The chapter borrows from Stephen Neill's 1957 work *The Unfinished Task*. Neill was an Anglican missionary, bishop, and linguist; he was also one of the earliest thinkers to discern the coming of "worldwide" Christianity and discuss its potential implication for missions. The chapter rehearses some of the arguments used by Neill in the late 1950s and repackages them for World Christianity in the twenty-first century. Chapter 6 pushes back on the assumption that the Western Church is in some sense the "savior" of the world. It provides a thought-provoking introduction to Christian missions, national pride, and racist policies, and briefly explores how attitudes of cultural and racial superiority have influenced the way some Christians have viewed the non-Western world in the twentieth century. In my own survey of the impressive body of literature on World Christianity, I was surprised by how little had been said about this topic. In chapter 7 I introduce readers to the new era of world missions in the twenty-first century. Due to the constraints of this project, I must leave some of the practical outworking to seasoned mission practitioners (and I do reference many such works in this book). I have generally tried to refrain from prophesying (forecasting the future of missions) or preaching (issuing imperatives)—or offering cookie-cutter formulas on missions in the twenty-first century. However, as someone who is committed to the "unfinished task" of world evangelism, readers will be able to detect my deeply held conviction that the Western church should adopt a new *world* view. I was unable to hide my own belief that the way forward in mission is working with our brothers and sisters in Christ around the world as equal partners in the gospel. This way of carrying out the *missio Dei* (mission of God),[13] working in cultural diversity while working cross-cultur-

13. I will sometimes use the expressions *missio Dei* (mission of God) and Great Commission synonymously only for literary variation. However, it may be helpful to point out for readers who are less conversant with mission

ally has the potential to transform the church, as well as the entire world.

NOTES ON STYLE, METHOD, AND LANGUAGE

This is a popular introduction informed by scholarly literature that has been rigorously peer-reviewed by the academic community, though it has been written in highly accessible prose. Primary sources from the period under investigation are also utilized throughout this short introduction. The work cites an array of journals, magazines, periodicals, newspapers, and draws from some archival materials. It is also sprinkled with an assortment of popular literary bric-a-brac that would be out of place in some academic writing. I have avoided the use of less reliable sources like crowd-sourced encyclopedias, popular histories, hagiographical works, tract literature, or secondary literature that has not been peer reviewed. The footnoting apparatus uses short-form citations, a style required by the publisher for popular writing. Readers (like me) who prefer seeing the full reference in the footnote apparatus can cross reference the work in the bibliography while reading. When reference is made to an entire work, the date of publication is given rather than the page number. Dates are also given for newspaper and periodical articles for quick reference. I have refrained from the pedantic citation of archival documents, though I have used some materials largely for the purpose of illuminating the larger narrative. I have also included anecdotes and stories in this work that would be largely out of place in a scholarly monograph. These latter flourishes are largely rhetorical (in an effort to make the reading more engaging) but they are also intended to show that

theology that beginning in the 1930s the Latin term *missio Dei* was used by scholars to show that the Great Commission given to the church (also known as the *mission ecclesiae*) is rooted in the person of God who has been on a mission since the fall, well before the New Testament church was established. The expression is used to emphasize that God is the one who is on a mission to restore suffering humanity and all of creation, though he now carries out his work through the church. For a brief discussion, see Bosch, *Transforming Mission*, 389–95.

my own thinking on World Christianity has been influenced by the many conversations I have had with Christians during periods of travel and research in Africa, Asia, and Latin America. As to historical method, I believe that it is still possible to understand the past, even if our knowledge is incomplete and our interpretations are flawed. For example, while it may not be possible to know what was going through the mind of every single one of the 7 million Christians living in Kenya in 1970, good historical spadework can still help us uncover things like the general attitudes of African church leaders toward Western missionaries in the 1970s. While we cannot pretend to possess a comprehensive knowledge of the past, even as we continually work to fill in the gaps, this does not mean we cannot know *something* about the past.[14]

This very short introduction on World Christianity has been published by an American press, written at a British academic study center, and pitched to a popular audience on both sides of the Atlantic. It is therefore likely to leave some readers feeling like I could have said more about some part of the world they care deeply about, or less about a Christian tradition they are not part of, while using words and idioms they are more familiar with. In a way that sounds almost comical, I have made every attempt to keep both feet firmly planted on five continents, while engaged with a wide body of current scholarly literature and writing in a way that is understandable for all readers. I have tried to avoid using language that is overtly Anglocentric even while carrying out much of my research in Cambridge. As someone who has spent a great deal of time in United Kingdom, I am keenly aware that there are significant differences between American and non-American readers that are nearly as wide as the Atlantic Ocean and far too extensive to enumerate here. I hope that my British friends and colleagues will not be gobsmacked by my occasional Americanisms. I have also been required by the publisher to conform to American standards in language and grammar, though I have tried to write with the awareness that many friends in other parts of the

14. For views that approximate my own, see Evans, *In Defense of History* (2000).

world will read this work. The more time I have spent in England the more I have come to appreciate the quip attributed to George Bernard Shaw (in various forms) that "the United States and Great Britain are two countries separated by a common language." As this is a cross-over work—written at an academic center, but for a popular audience—I have done my best to scotch as much technical jargon as possible from the manuscript without sacrificing precision. In the end, I hope that it is a blessing to many people around the world who are concerned about the unfinished task.

1

Shifting Southward

How the Gospel Is Turning the World Upside Down

"The era of Western Christianity has passed in our lifetimes, and the day of Southern Christianity is dawning."

—Philip Jenkins, *The Next Christendom*

After a long day of study in Cambridge I usually walk to an old pub across from Magdalene College where C. S. Lewis (1898–1963) would often repair for a pint with a colleague.[1] I consider this evening ritual a reward to myself for staying focused on research and writing throughout the day—especially when there are so many distractions that call out even in a place that is almost singularly devoted to study. At least that's how I justify my

1. Lewis and other literary friends like J. R. R. Tolkien met for many years in their "rooms" (rooms where professors lived in old colleges) and had conversations over a pint (or two) at the Eagle and Child pub during their time in Oxford together. When Lewis moved to Cambridge in 1954, he often enjoyed pints at the Pickerel Inn across from Magdalene College next to the river Cam. For a delightful popular introduction to these friendships, see Carter, *The Inklings* (1978).

pre-prandial pint—and I like to think that Lewis would heartily approve. It's not unusual to strike up a conversation with another academic in an old world pub, and when I tell someone I'm doing research in World Christianity it sometimes requires a lengthy explanation.[2] I recently told a fellow academic with a doctorate in aeronautics about the research I was doing on the history of Christianity in East Africa and he said: "Oh, yes! Isn't that the study of how Christianity fell into decline after Africans gained their independence from the British?" I smiled, remembering that I knew almost nothing about aeronautical engineering, and then replied, "Actually, it's quite the opposite. Christianity grew even more rapidly after decolonization." He was both astonished and intrigued.

I could recount dozens of similar conversations, not only with fellow academics, but also with Christian laypersons that are passionate about missions. If you didn't know that most Christians live in the non-Western world (the vast majority of them) and that the church actually grew more rapidly in Africa and Asia after decolonization, you are certainly not alone.[3] Even rocket scientists don't know about this remarkable turn of events! I've now become accustomed to the audible gasps in the room when I tell people that there are nearly three times as many Christians on the African continent than in the United States, Canada, and Greenland combined! The most recent data on World Christianity reports that in 2020 there were 267 million Christians in all of Northern America compared to 667 million followers of Christ in Africa![4] Many faithful church members, especially those in Northern America,

2. When I'm not teaching in some far-flung corner of the globe, or raising awareness for theological education in the non-Western world, I work at the Cambridge Centre for Christianity Worldwide (CCCW), a research center established during the nineteenth-century missionary movement in Cambridge. The Centre is devoted to "connecting Cambridge to the World" and promoting a better understanding of the nature of World Christianity: https://www.cccw.cam.ac.uk.

3. In my conversations with Christians in England and Scotland over the past decade or more, I have observed that European Christians are generally more informed on international developments, including the growth of Christianity in the non-Western world.

4. Johnson and Zurlo, *World Christian Encyclopedia* (2020), 4.

find it almost inconceivable when they learn that the world's largest mega churches are not in Houston, Dallas, Chicago, Atlanta, or Los Angeles; they are in Lagos (Nigeria), Harare (Zimbabwe), Nairobi (Kenya), Hyderabad (India), Surabaya (Indonesia), Rio de Janeiro (Brazil), and Seoul (South Korea). And the numbers aren't even close![5]

The Yale historian Lamin Sanneh (1942–2019) was born in West Africa and educated in the United States and England. He devoted most of his career to writing about Christianity in the non-Western world. Joel Carpenter is an academic whose work has largely focused on the history of Evangelicalism, a movement that has now expanded beyond the borders of the United States and Europe.[6] In the introduction to their collaborative work on Africa and the West in 2005 they observed that

> One of the most important and least examined changes in the world over the past century has been the rapid rise of Christianity in non-Western societies and cultures. In 1900, 80 percent of the world's professing Christians were Europeans or North Americas. Today, 60 percent of Christians live in the global South and East.[7]

Those words were written in 2005—some fifteen years ago. The percentage of Christians living in the Global South is now closing in on 70 percent and scholars are working overtime to explore these "least examined changes." The growth of the church in the non-Western world is not only remarkable, it is considered by leading experts to be one of the least understood subjects of our day.

A WORLD TOUR OF CHRISTIANITY

Christianity has always been a world religion, but it is now growing most rapidly in the world's Southern Hemispheres. Economists,

5. Bird, "The World's Largest Churches," Leadership Network.
6. Hutchinson and Wolffe, *A Short History of Global Evangelicalism* (2012).
7. Sanneh and Carpenter, *The Changing Face of Christianity*, vii.

sociologists, historians, and theologians are now using the term "Global South" to refer to the regions of Latin America, sub-Saharan Africa (Africa below the Sahara), Asia and Oceania (Australia and the Pacific Rim).[8] The vast majority of nations in the Southern Hemisphere are developing countries (with some notable exceptions), previously referred to as the Third World (though the latter expression is being used with less frequency because of its association with attitudes of Anglo-Saxon superiority).[9] During the twentieth century, the church in the Global South experienced unprecedented growth that shows no signs of slowing.[10] The "statistical center of gravity" (sometimes referred to as the "heartland" of Christianity) has shifted away from the West and moved into the southern regions of the globe.[11] If you were locating the new center of the church on the map of the world it would be in Africa—somewhere near Timbuktu![12]

This chapter provides a very short world tour of Christianity in the contemporary world, surveying the globe in the regions of Europe, Northern America, Latin America, Africa, Asia, and Oceania.[13] While ancient Christianity actually began in Western Asia and North Africa around the Mediterranean Basin, we will begin our modern overview in Europe and then cross the Atlantic to the New World before moving to the Global South where the church is now growing most rapidly. We will briefly touch on Oceania to make our journey complete. The brevity of this work does not allow for a treatment of Arabaphone Africa, the Middle East, and the small but vibrant Christianity communities that are

8. Dados and Connell, "The Global South," 12–13.

9. Tomlinson, "What Was the Third World?" 307–21.

10. Shaw, *Global Awakening* (2010).

11. Robert, "Shifting Southward," 50.

12. Johnson and Ross, "Christianity's Centre of Gravity, AD 33–2100," 52–53.

13. Scholars working in the field of World Christianity group the world into five regions (rather than continents) for the purposes of their research: Northern America (Greenland, Canada, and the United States), Latin America (Mexico, Central America, and South America), Europe, Asia, and Oceania (Australia, New Zealand, and the Pacific Islands).

present in those regions. Brief reference will be made to the history of Christianity on each continent, but this background is intended to give readers a better understanding of the contemporary scene. This is a brief survey of what is happening in the church around the world at the beginning of the twenty-first century.

Europe

"The faith is Europe. And Europe is the faith." That was how the Anglo-French writer Hilaire Belloc ended his 1920 work on Christianity in Europe.[14] Christianity has been part of European culture since the late first century, as the apostle Paul's correspondence with the churches in modern-day Greece and Italy attest. The European continent is rich in history and culture, and home to many of the oldest and most spectacular churches and monasteries in the world. Europe is the place of catacombs and cathedrals, the venerable residence of the bishop of Rome, the birthplace of the Protestant Reformation, the home of the worldwide Anglican Communion, and (if I may add from personal experience) it possesses a wealth of archival materials for the study of Christian history. Christianity spread from Jerusalem and moved to the West into Europe in the first century even as it continued to move East and South. Europe became largely Christianized by the year 1000 AD, and by the year 1500 AD (with the fall of Constantinople in 1453) it became the veritable heartland of the Christian faith. The Old World would remain the center of the Christian faith for the next 400 years.

During the twentieth century, Europe's hold on the faith began to atrophy. Increasing secularization in Western Europe and the heavy-hand of totalitarian regimes in Eastern Europe (suppressing Christian faith communities) noticeably weakened Christianity throughout the continent.[15] In Italy, where one would expect the Church of Rome to be most vibrant, 25 percent of

14. Belloc, *Europe and the Faith*, 261.

15. Coleman, "Christianity in Western Europe," 65–76.

professing Catholics attend mass. In Spain, 18 percent of Catholics routinely go to church; and in Germany and Austria 15 percent of Catholics are churchgoers. In France, where Christianity has been rooted since the second century, less than 12 percent of Catholics attend worship services on a given Sunday. When Pope John Paul II visited Paris in 1980 he complained, "Eldest daughter of the church, what have you done with your baptism?"[16] In the Protestant strongholds of Northern Europe church attendance is weaker. In Sweden, between 70 and 80 percent of young adults say they have no religious affiliation.[17] In Germany, the homeland of Martin Luther (1483–1586), less than 4 percent of Protestants affiliated with the Evangelical Church regularly attend worship services.[18] Across the English Channel, there are more encouraging signs, though fewer than 15 percent of adults and less than 3 percent of young people (under the age of twenty-four), now identify with the Church of England.[19]

The beautiful churches of Europe are still frequented by millions of visitors every year, but not for worship. As one British journalist put it:

> Like millions of people, I don't go to church, but I do go to churches—85% of the public visits a church every year. We regard them as the community's ritual forum, its museum, its art gallery, its concert hall, its occasional retreat for peace, consolation and mediations.[20]

There are tens of millions of faithful Christians in Europe, along with scores of vibrant Evangelical communities, and it is not

16. Sciolino, "Europeans Fast Falling Away from the Church," *New York Times*; Weigel, *Witness to Hope*, 366–77.

17. Sherwood, "'Christianity as Default Is Gone': The Rise of a Non-Christian Europe," *The Guardian*, March 21, 2018.

18. Schuster, "6 Facts about Catholic and Protestant Influence in Germany," *Deutsch Welle (DW)*.

19. Sherwood, "More Than Half of UK Population Has No Religion, Finds Survey," *The Guardian*; See also Ward, *A History of Global Anglicanism*, 296–318.

20. Jenkins, "England's Churches Can Survive—but the Religion Will Have to Go," *The Guardian*, October 22, 2015.

difficult to find Christian congregations that are engaged in active witness. About half of Europeans say they still believe in God, and many Orthodox, Catholic, Protestant, and Pentecostal Christians faithfully attend church.[21] In very recent years there has even been an increase in attendance at cathedral services in England.[22] (And on a personal note, one of the things I love most about Cambridge is the many churches and chapels that are open daily for prayer, reflection, and communion.) However, Europe is no longer "the faith."[23] There have been hopeful signs of Christian resurgence since the 1990s, and Eastern Europe may be entering a period of renewal aided in part by the break up of the Soviet Union. However, there are strong indications of decline across the continent, and Europe is no longer the statistical center of Christianity.[24] Vibrant Christian communities are persevering in exile and visible expressions of Christianity remain, but the era of European Christendom over.

North(ern) America[25]

Contrary to the popular notion that the church in Northern America is following European patterns, Christianity is experiencing modest growth in the New World. Christianity is an Old World transplant, and some of its cities and towns still bear witness to the priorities of European immigrants. One of my favorite views of Chicago is from atop the Skyway Toll Bridge (1958) that rises above the historic South Side and connects Northwest Indiana

21. Jacobson, *Global Gospel*, 128.

22. "Record Numbers of Visitors and Worshippers Flock to England's Cathedrals," The Church of England Research and Statistics.

23. Jenkins, *God's Continent*, 26–54; for analysis, see Brown, *The Death of Christian Britain* (2010).

24. Kuzmic, "Christianity in Eastern Europe," in Farhadian, *Introducing World Christianity*, 77–90.

25. Mexico is typically grouped with Latin America by demographers of World Christianity. The term Northern America (rather than North America) is used to refer to the regions north of Mexico, including the United States, Canada, and Greenland (though the terms are sometimes used interchangeably).

(my home for many years) to one of the largest cities in America. On a clear day (and such days occasionally occur!), one can see countless old steeples and spires in the distance, evoking images of America's patchwork immigrant history. During the nineteenth century and into the twentieth, millions of Europeans relocated to the New World and created communities around local churches in an effort to sustain their ethnic identities in a new land. Swedish Lutherans settled in Minnesota and Wisconsin, Scottish Presbyterians populated Nova Scotia (New Scotland), Dutch Reformed communities scattered throughout Michigan and Illinois, Moravian and German Baptists built towns along rivers in Ohio and Pennsylvania. Irish, Italian, and Polish Catholics created neighborhoods in New York, Boston, and Chicago. Old World immigrants and their children spread further South and West, planting their faith in the fertile soils of the New World and Christianity flourished in the free marketplace of religious ideas.[26] Christianity had room to grow and freedom to prosper in the New World—far away from European developments.

The history of religious disestablishment (separation from state control) is one of the reasons North American Christianity differs from its Old World counterpart. American ministers and churches have long been accustomed to competing for converts in the free market of religious ideas. Tocqueville had remarked in 1835 on the peculiar way in which American ministers were more political than priestly. As he put it, "You will be surprised to find a politician . . . where you expected to find a priest."[27] North American pastors may not always be known for deep theological reflection, but they are usually well versed in innovative management techniques, leadership principles, and technological trends. The worship services (including the sermons) of growing North American churches often have a populist flair that strike many

26. For helpful insights on why Christianity in North America has such a different ethos than Christianity in Europe, see Noll, *The Old Religion in a New World* (2002).

27. Tocqueville, *Democracy in America*, 335.

Europeans friends as odd.[28] Populist Christianity is all the rage in modern-day North America.

During the early twenty-first century there has been an uptick in the number of Northern Americans that are responding to polls regarding religious affiliation by saying that they have "none," a phenomenon known as "the rise of the religions 'nones.'"[29] However, while the percentage of people who are religiously unaffiliated (meaning they do not identify with a particular faith tradition) has been rising, the World Christian Database reports that the number of Christians in Northern American has slightly increased from 253 million in 2000 to some 267 million in 2020.[30] The rise of the religious "nones" is coinciding with a modest increase in the overall number of Christians. Although the percentage of the religiously unaffiliated has been increasing, the number of Christians in North America is still growing. The Catholic Church has been beleaguered by scandals and cover-ups, though the overall number of Catholics remain fairly stable due in part to Hispanic immigration from Latin American countries.[31] Mainline Protestant denominations (Episcopal, Methodist, Lutheran, and Presbyterian) have been losing members due in part to their liberal posture on social issues coupled with a dislike for modifying the liturgy to appeal to religious consumers.[32] The Evangelical offshoots of mainline churches with their ability to adapt to changing styles in the culture, as well as some congregations within mainline denominations with an Evangelical ethos, are continuing to grow.[33] Strict fundamentalist churches, those comprising Christians who parted ways with Billy Graham (1918–2018) and rejected the label

28. The classic scholarly analysis is found in Hatch, *The Democratization of American Christianity* (1991).

29. Lugo and Cooperman, "'Nones' on the Rise," *Pew Research Center*.

30. Johnson and Zurlo, *World Christian Encyclopedia*, 4.

31. Saad, "Catholics' Church Attendance Resumes Downward Slide," *Gallup*, April 9, 2018.

32. Stetzer, "If It Doesn't Stem Its Decline, Mainline Protestantism Has Just 23 Easters Left," *The Washington Post*, April 28, 2017.

33. Stone, "'Mainline' Churches Are Emptying." *Vox*, July 14, 2017.

Evangelical during the postwar period, have struggled to maintain their influence.[34] In stark contrast to fundamentalist Christians, the number of Evangelical Christians, which now includes the Pentecostal and non-Pentecostal faithful, continues to increase. Mega-churches in large cities are opening new campuses and inspiring a wave of innovative church-planting initiatives with significant appeal to younger Christians.[35] Christianity in Northern America has weakened in certain denominations and regions, but it is enjoying modest growth.[36]

Latin America

Over the last 100 years the center of Christianity's gravity has shifted southward. Latin America (Mexico, the Caribbean, Central America, and South America) was "conquered" for the faith during the Age of Discovery (ca. 1500–1800) by Spanish and Portuguese missionaries, who gained a reputation for carrying out their work in militant fashion.[37] Protestants attempts to conduct evangelistic work in Latin America during the same period were largely unsuccessful. John Calvin (1509–62), perhaps the most celebrated of Protestants, sent missionaries to Brazil in 1555, but the work soon ended in failure.[38] Between 1500 and 1900, Latin America was largely Roman Catholic, and Christianity was often harshly imposed on local populations by imperial authorities.

34. In the mid 1950s, fundamentalist leaders like John R. Rice, Bob Jones Sr., and Carl McIntire opposed Billy Graham's progressive Evangelicalism. These leaders garnered a wide following, creating a resurgent neo-fundamentalist movement that gained momentum in the 1960s through the 1970s. They adhered to strict separationist principles, including separation from Evangelical Christians who maintained fellowship with those that fundamentalists considered "liberal" or "modernist." An insider's perspective has been provided in Beale, *In Pursuit of Purity: American Fundamentalism Since 1850* (1986).

35. Smith, *American Evangelicalism: Embattled and Thriving* (1998).

36. Stanton, "New Harvard Study Says U.S. Christianity Is Not Shrinking, But Growing Stronger," *The Federalist*, January 22, 2018.

37. González and González, *Christianity in Latin America*, 12–63.

38. González and González, *Christianity in Latin America*, 186–87.

During the first half of the nineteenth century, at the same time that Latin American colonies were struggling for independence from Iberian powers, Protestant immigrants and mission agencies from the United States and the United Kingdom began spreading the Evangelical faith to various parts of Mexico, Central America, South America, and the Caribbean.[39] (Protestants mission societies had made gains in parts of the Caribbean from the 1790s.) By the year 1900, there were some 60 million Christians (Roman Catholics and Protestants) in Latin America, though between 1900 and 2020 the church grew exponentially, rising to more than 600 million adherents.[40] In 2013, as an ecclesiastical nod to the rapidly growing church in Latin America, the College of Cardinals elected an Argentinian to serve on the papal throne. Francis I became the first clergyman from the Southern Hemisphere to be elected to the Papal See.[41] The Bishop of Rome lives in Europe, but most of the people he shepherds live in Latin America and the Global South!

During the colonial period in Latin America (ca. 1500–1850), the Roman Catholic Church held a privileged position due to its identity with Spain and Portugal.[42] Only a handful of small Caribbean islands with cultural ties to Britain and the Netherlands remained predominantly Protestant.[43] However, during the twentieth century, Evangelical Protestants, especially those from the Pentecostal tradition, made significant gains in Latin America. Pentecostalism, an early-twentieth-century offshoot of Evangelicalism, is now the most rapidly growing church in Latin America—and the world.[44] Even large sections of the Catholic Church have embraced aspects of Pentecostal theology. By the beginning of the

39. González and González, *Christianity in Latin America*, 184–239.

40. Zurlo, "World Christianity and Mission 2020," 17.

41. Gibson, "The Story Behind Pope Francis' Election," *USA Today*, March 16, 2013.

42. Mariz and Martín, "Christianity in South America, 1910–2010," 186–87.

43. Sands, "Christianity in the Caribbean, 1910–2010" in Johnson and Ross, *Atlas of Global Christianity*, 178–81.

44. Anderson, *To the Ends of the Earth: Pentecostalism and the Transformation of World Christianity* (2013).

twenty-first century, more than one third of Christians in Peru, and nearly half of all Christians in Brazil, identified with Pentecostal Christianity.[45] While Roman Catholicism still predominates, Evangelical Protestants are growing more rapidly.[46] The magnificent statute, Christ the Redeemer, overlooking the city of Rio de Janeiro serves as a fitting monument to the ascendancy of modern-day Christianity in the Global South.[47] Christianity in Latin America has been born again![48]

Africa

In 1900 there were 9 million Christians on the entire continent of Africa. A little more than 100 years later, the number of Christians in African numbered more than 667 million![49] When discussing Christianity in Africa, it is important to remember that Christianity is not a Western religion. The church has had a long presence on the African continent, tracing its lineage to the earliest Christians. On the day of Pentecost (ca. 30 AD) there were present in Jerusalem "God-fearing Jews *from every nation*" [emphasis mine] and among their number were people from the African regions of "Egypt and parts of Libya."[50] The "Ethiopian eunuch, an important official in charge of all the treasury of Candace, queen of the Ethiopians" was converted to Christ and baptized while on his journey back to Africa.[51] In the first century Christianity spread to Africa through the Jewish-Christian diaspora (Jews dispersed throughout the world who had converted to Christianity). Many of the early church fathers from the second through the fifth centuries were

45. González and González, *Christianity in Latin America*, 283.

46. González and González, *Christianity in Latin America*, 270–96; Johnstone, *Operation World*, 47–48.

47. Murray, "Christ the Redeemer Statue, Mount Corcovado, Brazil," *Encyclopedia Britannica*.

48. Hartch, *The Rebirth of Latin American Christianity* (2014).

49. Johnson and Zurlo, *World Christian Encyclopedia* (2020), 4.

50. Acts 2:5–10.

51. Acts 2:26–40.

Africans, including Tertullian of Carthage (155–240), Origen of Alexandria (185–254), Athanasius of Alexandria (328–373), and Augustine of Hippo (354–430). Twentieth-century archaeological evidence has revealed the presence of vibrant Christian communities spanning much of North Africa through the year 900 AD. Vibrant Christian communities were also present in cities and towns along the Nile stretching from the Mediterranean Sea in the north, to as far south as Khartoum (North Sudan).[52] Even after the collapse of Christianity in Nubia (North Sudan) around the tenth century, the old faith remained firmly rooted in Ethiopia from the fourth century up to the present day, giving inspiration to many twentieth-century independent African churches.[53] (Many African independent churches used the term "Ethiopian Church" in the early twentieth century.) The church is not new to Africa and it is simply wrongheaded to dismiss Christianity as a Western import. The revival of Christianity in Africa today is best described as the reawakening of a non-Western religion.[54] The African church has had a profound influence on the numerical growth and theological development of the church for 2,000 years.[55]

While Christianity has been present in Africa since the first century up to the present period, beginning in the 1790s there was a revival of Protestant and Catholic missionary work on the continent, especially in sub-Saharan Africa.[56] Portuguese, Spanish, and French Catholics worked along the coastal waterways from the late 1400s, but they seldom ventured inland.[57] During the nineteenth century a new generation of explorers, like David Livingstone (1813–73) and Henry Morton Stanley (1841–1904) inspired missionaries (and settlers) to venture further inland by following new maps created by the Royal Geographic Society. In an effort to

52. Sundkler and Steed, *A History of the Church in Africa*, 7–38.

53. Shaw, *The Kingdom of God in Africa*, 91–106.

54. Bediako, *Christianity in Africa: The Renewal of a Non-Western Religion* (1995).

55. Oden, *How Africa Shaped the Christian Mind* (2010).

56. Hastings, *The Church in Africa*, 242–58.

57. Sundkler and Steed, *A History of the Church in Africa*, 100–123.

survive in Africa's vast interior, mission societies created supply chains comprised of "mission stations" along navigable waterways and trade routes. By the twentieth century an indigenous African church had begun to experience scalable growth in much of Tropical Africa.[58] During decolonization (ca. 1940s through the 1990s), when African leaders led freedom revolts and told the white man to "scram from Africa,"[59] secular thinkers and some mission leaders feared that the church would "fall apart."[60] However, the African church grew even more rapidly in the second half of the twentieth century during decolonization. By 1970, there were 140 million Christians on the continent while some thirty years later that number had more than doubled to 382 million. At the current rate of growth, by the year 2050 the church in Africa is expected to exceed an astonishing 1.3 billion believers![61] The diversity of the church in Africa reflects the cosmopolitan nature of World Christianity, the variety of mission organizations that have been working throughout the vast continent, and the mushrooming of African Independent Churches (AICs). Today there are high concentrations of Orthodox Christians in Egypt and Ethiopia (as well as some Evangelicals), an array of Evangelicals from varied denominations in East Africa, along with many Roman Catholics, and a large number of Roman Catholics and Anglo-Catholics in the Democratic Republic of Congo and parts of Francophone Africa. There are older Protestants denominations along with new African independent churches, including Zionist Christians, in South Africa, Zambia, Namibia, and Zimbabwe. In West Africa, Pentecostalism is growing rapidly, though an emphasis on the work of the Spirit is diffused throughout most denominations and groups on the continent. The Anglican tradition is vibrant throughout Anglophone Africa, and it is decidedly Evangelical.

58. Groves, *The Planting of Christianity in Africa*, 195–237.

59. Tom Mboya (1930–60) in Meredith, *The Fate of Africa*, 29.

60. Sanneh, *Whose Religion is Christianity?* 15; The expression "things fall apart" was popularized in the classic African novel Chinua Achebe, *Things Fall Apart* (1994), first published in 1958.

61. Zurlo and Johnson, *World Christian Encyclopedia* (2020), 4.

Christianity has been present in Africa for 2,000 years, but in the twentieth century the African church has now become the new heartland of the Christian faith.

Asia

Christianity in Asia, from Jerusalem to Jakarta, has experienced revival during the past 100 years. In 1900 there were approximately 21 million Christians scattered across the continent of Asia, the most populous region in the world. By 1970, the number of Christians had increased to 95 million, reaching nearly 280 million by the year 2000.[62] As in Africa, Christianity has been present in Asia for 2,000 years. The church was born in Jerusalem in 33 AD and became firmly planted in Western Asia by the early third century. The oldest surviving house-church dates to about 232 AD (some 100 years before Constantine) and was discovered by archaeologists at Dura Europos on the Euphrates, midway between Aleppo (Syria) and Baghdad (Iraq).[63] Several ancient sources, including the well-known *Acts of Thomas* (ca. 200 AD) recount the missionary exploits of the apostle Thomas in India, and the historical record indicates the early establishment of vibrant Christian communities in South Asia that flourished well into the sixth century.[64] Contrary to our mental maps that typically imagine an immediate Western shift of the church (from Jerusalem to Rome) at the end of the first century, the church in Western Asia (Armenia, Iran, Iraq, Israel, Syria, and Turkey) and Southern Asia (the Indian Subcontinent) was at least as large as the church in Europe in the year 800.[65] Only in the fifteenth century did the church in Western Asia begin its slow demise, eventually being reduced to mere obscuration.[66]

62. Johnson and Zurlo, *World Christian Encyclopedia* (2004), 4.

63. "Dura Europos," in Cross and Livingstone, *Dictionary of the Christian Church*, 516–17.

64. Bundy, "Early Asian and East African Christianities,"120–21; Frykenberg, "India," 147–56.

65. Jenkins, *The Lost History of Christianity*, 1–70.

66. Jenkins, *The Lost History of Christianity*, 97–138.

In the early 1500s, Catholic missionaries wended their way over oceans and along the Silk Road to South Asia, Southeast Asia, and East Asia. Protestant missionaries began arriving in the eighteenth and nineteenth centuries to plant (or re-plant) Christianity. As in Africa, Roman Catholics and Protestants from varied societies and agencies, both denominational (e.g., Roman Catholic Jesuits, the Church Missionary Society, the Baptist Missionary Society, the American Board of Commissioners for Foreign Missions) and non-denominational (e.g., the China Inland Mission, the Oriental Missionary Society) spread throughout the continent and undertook bold initiatives in India, China, Korea, Vietnam, Japan, Indonesia, and neighboring countries.[67] Christianity in Asia, rooted in the soils of ancient Syria and Mesopotamia, would experience a revival in the twentieth century, though the main centers of growth would be in the East, South, and Southeastern regions of Asia.

More than half of the world's 7.5 billion people live in Asia, which is now home to some of the world's largest Evangelical mega churches. Calvary Temple in Hyderabad, India has a gathering space that is able to seat some 35,000 worshippers. The worship center is filled to capacity five times on Sunday beginning with a service at six o'clock in the morning.[68] The number of Christians in India was estimated at 20 million in 1970, and is expected to increase to more than 60 million by 2025.[69] Though it is a small number compared to the country's population of more than 1.3 billion people, the gospel is shining brightly in large cities and small villages through vibrant church communities and the efforts of indigenous workers and collaborative mission efforts. Several states in northeast India, including Manipur, Mizoram, Meghalaya, and Nagaland, are predominantly Christian, with flourishing church communities and Bible colleges, and an estimated 40,000

67. Tiedemann, "China and Its Neighbours," 373–90.

68. Jeremy Weber, "Incredible Indian Christianity: A Special Report on the World's Most Vibrant Christward Movement," *Christianity Today*, October 21, 2016.

69. Daughrity and Athyal, *Understanding World Christianity: India*, 170–73; Ross, *Christianity in South and Central Asia*, 448.

indigenous Christian missionaries from India are working to spread the gospel to the neighboring countries of Pakistan, Nepal, Bhutan, and Bangladesh.[70] The Yoido Full Gospel Church in Seoul, South Korea, boasts a membership of nearly 500,000 people (though a reported 800,000 people attend services) and mobilizes some 600 new missionaries every year. Many of the church's full-time workers are sent to North Korea and neighboring Asian countries.[71] South Korea now sends out more missionaries to foreign lands than any country in the world except the United States.[72] Indonesia, the nation with the largest population of Muslims in the world, experienced a Christian resurgence beginning in the 1960s and is now home to vibrant Christian communities with large congregations that are engaged in evangelistic work.[73] More than 140,000 worshippers attend Bethany Church of God in Surabaya, Indonesia each Sunday, while there are Evangelical churches on Bali and Jakarta with weekly attendances that exceed 8,000.[74]

In China, the church continued to grow following the Communist Revolution (1946–49) when foreign missionaries were expelled from the country. After 1949, the Chinese Protestant clergyman Y. T. Wu (1893–1979), who was educated at Columbia University and Union Theological Seminary, provided significant impetus for the indigenization of the church through the Three-Self Patriotic Movement.[75] The Chinese church emerged from a period of oppression during the Cultural Revolution (1966–77) poised for a new era of flourishing in the final quarter of the twentieth century.[76] *Times* correspondent David Aikman recalls meeting

70. Frykenberg, *Christianity in India*, 5.

71. "O Come All Ye Faithful," *The Economist*, November 1, 2007.

72. Moll, "Missions Incredible," *Christianity Today*, March 1, 2006.

73. Aritonang and Steenbrink, *A History of Christianity in Indonesia*, 203–26.

74. Bird, "The World's Largest Churches," Leadership Network.

75. Wangzhi, "Y. T. Wu: A Christian Leader under Communism," in Bays, *Christianity in China*, 338–52.

76. Wickeri, *Reconstructing Christianity in China: K. H. Ting and the Chinese Church*, 167–98, 285–332.

only a few Christians in the 1980s during his work as the Beijing Bureau Chief, but noted that things had changed by the 1990s. As he put it: "[In the 1990s] I began to meet intellectuals, academics, social scientists, businessmen, artists, and musicians, some of them party members, most of them not, who were unmistakably Christian believers, and who acknowledged this privately."[77] The number of Christians in China is difficult to estimate. The *World Christianity Encyclopedia* reported that there were about 80 million Christians in China in 2000 and estimated numbers to exceed 200 million by 2050.[78] *Operation World* gives a 2010 estimate of 105 million, while the *Atlas of Global Christianity* reported 115 million Christians in the same year.[79] It appears safe to say that the Christian population in China now exceeds more than 100 million, with an estimated 10 million young converts entering the church every year. Christian leaders in China have even embraced a vision to canvas the continent by taking the gospel "Back to Jerusalem" in an effort to complete the Great Commission.[80] The aim of the Back to Jerusalem Movement is "to evangelize the unreached peoples from [the] eastern provinces of China, westwards towards Jerusalem."[81] The number of believers on the entire continent of Asia has reached approximately 378 million, now exceeding the number of Christians in all of North America. At the current rate of rapid growth, the church in Asia is expected to exceed 400 million in 2025 and 570 million by the year 2050.[82] The Asian church has experienced a new birth and is now teeming with hundreds of millions of Christians with a bold vision to spread the gospel across the continent and out to the rest of the world.

77. Aikman, *Jesus in Beijing*, 8.

78. Johnson and Zurlo, *World Christian Encyclopedia* (2020), 195.

79. Johnstone, *Operation World*, 215; Johnson and Ross, *Atlas of Global Christianity*, 140.

80. Yun et al., *Back to Jerusalem: Three Chinese House Church Leaders Share Their Vision to Complete the Great Commission* (2005).

81. Interview with Paul Hattaway, "A Captivating Vision: Why Chinese House Churches May Just End Up Fulfilling the Great Commission," *Christianity Today*, April 1, 2004 ; "What Is 'Back to Jerusalem'?" *Back to Jerusalem*.

82. Zurlo, "World Christianity and Mission 2020," 17.

Oceania

Christianity in Oceania, the region comprising Australia, New Zealand, the Pacific Islands (Micronesia, Melanesia, and Polynesia), and Papua New Guinea is not in steep decline, though its future remains uncertain.[83] Missionaries arrived in Oceania in the sixteenth century through Roman Catholic societies travelling to the South Pacific with colonial governments who were seeking to extend Spanish influence. In the late eighteenth century, the Church Missionary Society (Anglican) arrived, becoming especially influential in Australia and New Zealand. The London Missionary Society (Congregational) and missionaries of the Free Presbyterian Church were especially active in the Pacific Islands.[84] By 1900, there were some 4 million Christians in Oceania, a number that increased to 25 million by 2017.[85] Nearly 75 percent of Oceania's more than 35 million inhabitants identify with the Christian faith.[86] Some parts of Oceania experienced a Pacific awakening during the twentieth century. The percentage of Christians in Melanesia, which includes Vanuatu, the Solomon Islands, Fiji, and Papua New Guinea, increased from 15 percent of the population in 1910, to more than 90 percent by 2010, while in Micronesia the percentage of the faithful grew from 77 percent to more than 92 percent during the same period.[87] Christianity in Polynesia has remained relatively unchanged since 1910, with more than 95 percent of its nearly 700,000 inhabitants identifying

83. Massam, "Christian Churches in Australia, New Zealand and the Pacific, 1914–1970," in Hugh Mcleod, *The Cambridge History of World Christianity, Vol. 9*, 252–61.

84. For an overview, see Hilliard, "Australia and the Pacific," in Adrian Hastings, *A World History of Christianity*, 508–35.

85. Zurlo et al., "World Christianity and Mission 2020," 17; cf. Johnson and Zurlo, *World Christian Encyclopedia* (2020), 4.

86. Johnstone, *Operation World*, 84–85; "Christianity in Oceania," in Johnson and Ross, *Atlas of Global Christianity*, 194–95.

87. "Christianity in Oceania," in Johnson and Ross, *Atlas of Global Christianity*, 194.

with the Christian faith.[88] Meanwhile, Australia and New Zealand, the two most populous countries in Oceania, are becoming more secular. Christians represented 97 percent of the population of Australia and New Zealand in 1910, but that percentage dropped to 75 percent by 2010. This demographic shift has been due to an increase in the number of agnostics and atheists, as well an influx of immigrants from Southeast Asia who identify as Muslim, Buddhist, or Sikh.[89] However, the rise of secularism and religious pluralism in Australia and New Zealand has been largely offset by the growth of Christianity in the Pacific Islands of Oceania. While the majority of Pacific Islanders would identify themselves as Christians, waves of secularism and religious pluralism are altering the religious landscape.

GOD IS NOT DEAD

During the 1960s Western sociologists and theologians were debating the secularization thesis—the idea that the modern world was becoming increasingly secular. In 1961, the French theologian Gabriel Vahanian (1927–2012) published his now infamous book, *The Death of God: The Culture of our Post-Christian Era*. As a theologian, Vahanian was not asserting that God was actually dead (that there was no God). Instead, he was arguing that the modern world had entered a post-Christian era.[90] A few prominent theologians attempted new ways of responding to the perceived threat of secularization by constructing what became known as "Death of God Theology."[91] On April 4, 1966, *Time* magazine ran a sensational piece covering the conversation. "Is God Dead?" was printed in bold red on the issue's front cover. Luminaries of the

88. "Christianity in Polynesia, 1910–2010," in Johnson and Ross, *Atlas of Global Christianity*, 206–7.

89. "Christianity in Australia/New Zealand, 1910–2010," in Johnson and Ross, *Atlas of Global Christianity*, 198–99.

90. Vos, review of *The Death of God*, by Gabriel Vahanian, 76–77.

91. Gundry, "Death of God Theology," 301–2.

Western world believed that Christianity and religious fervor were in decline on a global scale.

As it turns out, God was not dead in the 1960s and the world was not becoming more secular. Most scholars, secular and religious, were simply so preoccupied with developments in the Western world that they failed to cast a wider gaze. The prominent Austrian sociologist Peter Berger (1929–2017), who embraced the secularization thesis in the 1960s and 1970s, said in 2014 that when he started out doing sociology of religion—"everyone else had the same idea [that the world was becoming more secular]."[92] In 1968 Berger had predicted that "by the 21st century, religious believers are likely to be found only in small sects, huddled together to resist a worldwide secular culture."[93] Nearly fifty years later Berger was forced to set the record straight: "The world today is not heavily secularized." Noting the exception of Europe he observed that "the rest of the world is massively religious. In some areas of the world, more religious than ever."[94]

At the beginning of the twenty-first century there are more than 2.5 billion Christians in the world, and nearly 70 percent of the faithful live in the Global South. The demographic center of Christianity is no longer in the Western world. Christianity is visibly present in Europe, still vibrant in North America, but growing most rapidly in Latin America, Africa, and Asia. As Philip Jenkins put it in 2003, "The era of Western Christianity has passed in our lifetimes, and the day of Southern Christianity is dawning. The fact of change is undeniable: it has happened, and will continue to happen."[95] To borrow from the book of Acts, the world has been "turned upside down."[96]

And who is keeping track of these remarkable changes?

92. Peter Berger, cited in Thuswaldner, "A Conversation with Peter L. Berger: 'How My Views Have Changed,'" 16–21.

93. Peter Berger, cited in, "A Bleak Outlook Is Seen for Religion," *New York Times*, February 25, 1968.

94. Berger in Thuswaldner, "A Conversation with Peter L. Berger," 16–21.

95. Jenkins, *The Next Christendom*, 3.

96. Noll, "Turning the World Upside Down: The Coming of Global Christianity," *Books & Culture*.

2

Counting Every Soul on Earth

How We Know So Much about World Christianity

"Ex Africa semper aliquid novi."
(Out of Africa [there is] always something new.)

—Pliny the Elder (23–70 AD)

THE RAPID GROWTH OF Christianity in the non-Western world during the modern period is so remarkable that it may even appear doubtful to some readers. There are now over 600 million Christians in Latin America! There are 667 million Christians in Africa, increasing to more than 1.3 billion by 2050! The number of believers in Asia is expected to exceed well over half a billion people well before 2050! There are scores of mega churches throughout Asia that dwarf the largest congregations in North America. Wow! I realize that for many people, especially those in North America, these are almost unbelievable numbers. That is one reason I have devoted a full chapter to the work of a few of the most fascinating people in the world some readers may have never heard of. They are impressive in their accomplishments, but the nature of their work requires them to spend extensive time carrying out research in remote regions of the world, far removed from public fanfare. As a result of their extensive research in the non-Western world we are learning about the status of the global church and we are gaining greater insights on *how* Christianity grew so rapidly during the twentieth century. The work these researchers are doing is not only transforming the way people understand the world, it is, as will be explained, also influencing mission strategy. In short, I want readers to get to know the real Dr. "Indiana" Joneses who are working in the field of World Christianity.

OUT OF AFRICA

The study of World Christianity was pioneered by the efforts of two British intellectuals with Oxbridge pedigrees and a Yale professor "summoned from the margin" of the tiny African nation of Gambia. "Out of Africa" came something new. Andrew Walls (b. 1928), David Barrett (1927–2011), and Lamin Sanneh (1942–2019) have changed the way people now understand the nature of Christianity around the world. Their work has also inspired established and emerging scholars to turn their attention to the growth of the church in the non-Western world. In 2007, *Christianity Today* referred to Andrew Walls as "the most important person you don't know."[1] He is a mild-mannered gentleman, now in his 90s, who is loved by students and colleagues alike. The bespectacled professor dons an old tweed jacket, sports a full grey beard, and speaks with a gentle but confident Scottish brogue. When I first met Walls, his mannerisms reminded me (oddly enough) of Dr. Jones, the father of "Indiana" Jones, played by the Scottish actor Sean Connery (b. 1930). Born in New Milton, England, in 1928, Walls graduated from Exeter College, Oxford at the age of twenty. Upon finishing his undergraduate degree, he undertook doctoral work in early Christianity with the Oxford patristic[2] scholar Frank Leslie Cross

1. Stafford, "Historian Ahead of His Time," *Christianity Today*, February 8, 2007.

2 Patristics is the sub-discipline of Christian history that is concerned with

(1900–1968). In 1957, Walls moved to West Africa to work as a lecturer in church history at the Fourah Bay College in Freetown, Sierra Leone, an institution founded in 1827 by CMS missionaries for training African clergy. In 1962, he was appointed the head of the religious department at the University of Nigeria, where he served until 1965, just before the outbreak of the Nigerian Civil War (1967–70).

Walls had an epiphany not long after his arrival in West Africa. He witnessed first hand the rapidly growing Christian communities around him and realized that the African church was already significantly larger than his own church in Great Britain! As a historian he wanted to gain a better understanding of the growth and nature of African Christianity, but where would he find sources for such a task? On his excursions outside the classroom he was astonished to find well-preserved archives in old African churches, some dating back for several centuries.[3] Recall that Roman Catholic missionaries had begun work in West Africa in the late 1400s and the Protestant Church Missionary Society (established in 1799) had been working in the region since the early nineteenth century. By the mid-1800s there were well-established Catholic and Protestant church communities throughout West Africa with a lengthy history that was simply waiting to be unearthed![4] (By comparison, Christianity in East Africa would mature later.) Walls' fieldwork in old churches opened his eyes to African leaders, revival movements, and liturgical innovations (worship styles) that were virtually unknown to the Western church. When he returned to Scotland in 1966 to teach church history at the University of Aberdeen he realized he had to completely change the course syllabus because of his research. Church history, he came to realize, was so much larger than the movement of Christianity from Jerusalem to Rome to Edinburgh—where it died a slow death in Scotland before making its way across the pond to North America. (This

the writings of the early church fathers (ca. 100–451 AD).

3 Stafford, "Historian Ahead of His Time," *Christianity Today*, February 8, 2007.

4. Sundkler and Steed, *A History of the Church in Africa*, 182.

was how Walls exaggerated the way courses were designed in the 1960s.) To use his words, the Scottish academic wanted to abandon the teaching of "clan history" and replace it with the teaching of "church history."[5] He also wanted to move beyond the study of Western missionaries and their work (something he still deemed important) in order to examine the actual church community in Africa, Asia, and the non-Western world. The problem was that historians had been so preoccupied with the study of church history in Europe and North America that few really understood what was actually happening in the non-Western world.

Walls began clearing a path for other scholars to study what became known as World Christianity. In 1967, after his return to Scotland to teach at Aberdeen, he founded the *The Journal of Religion in Africa (JRA)*, and in 1970 he was promoted to serve as head of religious studies. He slowly transformed the way church history was being taught and written. During the 1970s, he attracted talented academics to join the teaching staff at Aberdeen, including Harold W. Turner (1911–2002), Adrian Hastings (1929–2001), and Lamin Sanneh (see below), who all became notable historians and influential leaders in the field of World Christianity. Walls also mentored non-Western doctoral students who went on to make significant contributions in history and theology, including the well-known African theologian Kwame Bediako (1945–2008). In 1982, the Scottish professor established the Centre for the Study of Christianity in the Non-Western world at Aberdeen, subsequently relocated to the University of Edinburgh in 1986. The Centre accrued massive collections of secondary and primary source materials from Africa, Asia, and Latin America for the study of non-Western Christianity. (Many of these primary source materials came from mission societies.) In 2009, under the direction of the Cambridge scholar Brian Stanley, the name of the Centre was changed to The Centre for the Study of World Christianity.[6] Andrew Walls changed the way historians were looking at the world.

5. Walls, "Eusebius Tries Again," 107–8.

6. Stanley, "Founding the Centre for the Study of Christianity in the Non-Western World," 51–59.

The church was much larger and even more diverse than almost anyone had realized.[7]

David Barrett (1927–2011) was born in northern Wales, and graduated from Cambridge in 1948 with a degree in aeronautics. In 1954 he became an ordained minister in the Church of England and soon left for Kenya to serve as a missionary during the Mau Mau Conflict (ca. 1952–56). While on leave in the United States in 1965, Barrett undertook further studies at Union Theological Seminary, remaining in New York to undertake doctoral work at Columbia University.[8] As both a trained scientist and an experienced missionary, Barrett became fascinated with the "social scientific study of religion" in Africa.[9] In the course of his doctoral studies, he returned to East Africa to undertake field research on the status of Christianity across the African continent. Using Nairobi as his base, Barrett travelled across the vast continent of Africa and toured nearly every country. He visited crowded cities and rural towns, meeting with church leaders, denominational representatives, and university officials, and in the process amassing vast collections of stories and statistics on mission-established churches and African Independent Churches (AICs).[10] In 1968, Oxford published his doctoral work under the title *Schism and Renewal in Africa: An Analysis of 6,000 Contemporary Religious Movements*. ("Schism" in the title is a reference to the thousands of churches that broke with mission-established churches, often in rebellion of mission control.) His published work thrust him onto the scene as an expert on contemporary Christianity in Africa. Barrett's next major project was even more ambitious. Over a thirteen-year period, between 1968 and 1981, he travelled to 212 of the world's 223 countries and territories to conduct actual

7. Johnstone, *The Church is Bigger Than You Think* (2005).

8. Johnson, "David B. Barrett: Missionary Statistician," 30–32.

9. Zurlo, "David B. Barrett, 1927–2011," *Dictionary of African Christian Biography* (2017).

10. African independent churches (AICs) are independent Christian denominations that broke away from mission-established churches for various reasons.

fieldwork on the history and status of World Christianity.[11] His groundbreaking research was published by Oxford in 1982 under the title *World Christian Encyclopedia (WCE)* and was praised by the secular academic community as an unrivaled achievement. Barrett's oversized 1,000-page encyclopedia covered more than 20,000 denominations and included a history of Christianity in every country from the early church to the twentieth century! His research was hailed by *Time* magazine as "a miracle from Nairobi."[12] The second edition of the *WCE* was expanded to 1,700 pages and published in 2001, while an updated third edition was released in early 2020. Barrett laid the groundwork for the statistical analysis and demographic study of World Christianity.

The third pioneer in the field of World Christianity was Lamin Sanneh (1942–2019), who served as the D. Willis Professor of World Christianity at Yale until his death in 2019.[13] He was born on the small island of Georgetown in Gambia (West Africa) and became a convert to Christianity as a young teenager. He was greatly influenced by the mission school he attended as a child and recalls being deeply moved by the works of C. S. Lewis, which he stumbled upon at a supermarket in Banjul (the capital of Gambia).[14] Sanneh excelled in his studies in primary and secondary school and became the recipient of an academic scholarship funded by the U.S. Department of Education to attend university in the United States.[15] He completed his undergraduate studies at the exclusive Union College in New York before moving to England to do graduate work in Arabic and Islamic studies at the University of Birmingham (England).[16] While studying in England he was assigned to the theology department and baptized his study of Arabic and Islam with a full immersion in Christian theology,

11. Zurlo, "A Miracle from Nairobi," 2.

12. Ostling and Matheson, "Counting Every Soul on Earth: Miracle from Nairobi: The First Census of All Religions," *Time*, May 3, 1982.

13. Sanneh, *Summoned from the Margin* (2012).

14. Sanneh, *Summoned from the Margin*, 111.

15. Sanneh, *Summoned from the Margin*, 121.

16. Sanneh, *Summoned from the Margin*, 149.

African church history, and missions history. As a talented young scholar, Sanneh was beginning to formulate ideas that he would explore in many of his later works. His research was challenging the widely accepted scholarly consensus that Christianity was simply another cog in the colonial machinery that was used for the oppression of non-Western people. He had keenly observed that the end of colonial rule in the non-Western world had not meant the decline of Christianity, but its resurgence. As he would put it later: "The end of colonial rule removed obstacles in the path of Christian conversion, allowing the religion to commence the indigenous resurgence that was to distinguish its post-Western phase."[17] For Sanneh, the relationship between European colonialism and Christianity was more complex than he had been led to believe. His research was beginning to push back on the narrative that Christianity had enslaved Africans. It was actually advancing the hypothesis that Christianity may have actually contributed to the liberation of non-Western people.

Sanneh's intellectual journey continued during his doctoral studies at the School of Oriental and Africa Studies (SOAS) at the University of London. He enjoyed the academic rigors of working under the guidance of Roland Oliver (1923–2014), a pioneer in the academic study of African history and the editor of the *Cambridge History of Africa* and the *Oxford History of East Africa*.[18] Upon completing his doctoral work, the young scholar from Gambia returned to Africa to teach at the Fourah Bay College in Freetown, Sierra Leone (the same university where Walls had taught in the 1950s). He later moved to the University of Ghana and carried out research on the history of Christian-Muslim relations in Africa, while also working in the classroom as a young lecturer.[19] Although Sanneh had converted from Islam to Christianity, his life-long friendships with Muslim clerics, his intimate familiarity with the history of Christian-Muslim relations in Africa, and his fluency in Arabic, positioned him to explore the problem of

17. Sanneh, *Summoned from the Margin*, 168.

18. Oliver, *In the Realms of Gold: Pioneering in African History* (1997).

19. Sanneh, *Summoned from the Margin*, 211.

Christian-Muslim relations in the modern world.[20] In 1978, he was invited to a permanent teaching post at the University of Aberdeen (Scotland) where he became friends with Andrew Walls, who was then teaching in the church history department.[21] While preparing for lectures in African Christianity, Sanneh was struck by how often Christian missionaries had been misunderstood in the scholarly literature. He was impressed by the commitment of missionaries to engage in translating the Scriptures into vernacular African languages. He was "dumbfounded" by his discovery that Christian witness was not an effort to impose Western culture on unsuspecting Africans, even if missionaries at times failed to fully appreciate African culture. (He contrasted this with his experience as a Muslim, where conversion usually required assimilation into a particular culture.) On the contrary, the efforts of Western missionaries to "translate the Christian message" (a popular Sanneh refrain) into vernacular languages actually had the effect of preserving and renewing African cultures. In his words, "Christianity is a form of indigenous empowerment by virtue of vernacular translation."[22] Here was the genesis to the work for which he would become most widely known, *Translating the Message: The Missionary Impact on Culture.*[23] Sanneh was arguing against the conventional scholarly wisdom that Christianity was a form of Western imperialism, a cultural straightjacket that imposed the gospel on non-Western people and required them to abandon their cherished cultural identities and idioms. On the contrary, as he put it, "Christianity helped Africans to become renewed Africans, not remade Europeans."[24] Sanneh preferred the use of the term World Christianity over Global Christianity, admitting they were interchangeable, but arguing that the latter expression had

20. See for example, Sanneh, *Beyond Jihad: The Pacifist Tradition in West African Islam* (2016).

21. Sanneh, *Summoned from the Margin*, 214–15.

22. Sanneh, *Summoned from the Margin*, 217.

23. Sanneh, *Translating the Message: The Missionary Impact on Culture* (1989).

24. Sanneh, *Whose Religion Is Christianity?* 43.

connotations with imperialism and placed the emphasis on global influences in commerce, technology, and the arts, thus "dwarfing" (as he put it) the importance of local or indigenous faith.[25] After a short teaching stint at Harvard in the late 1980s, Sanneh moved to Yale in 1989, where he helped found the Yale-Edinburgh Group with Andrew Walls in 1992.[26] The Yale-Edinburgh Group, bolstered by generous funding from Pew Charitable Trusts, has served as a vibrant academic community fostering collaborative research in the field of World Christianity.[27] Andrew Walls, David Barrett, and Lamin Sanneh were key leaders in the formation of a new field of study that has become known as World Christianity.[28]

ADVANCES IN WORLD CHRISTIANITY

A growing community of seasoned academics and early-career scholars are now working in study centers and universities conducting research, writing books, churning out articles and teaching courses on World Christianity. The Centre for the Study of World Christianity at the University of Edinburgh (referred to earlier) has been led since 2009 by the British historian Brian Stanley (b. 1953), who is considered by many to be the world's leading expert on Christian missions and the study of Christianity in the non-Western world. His 1992 path-breaking work, *The Bible and the Flag: Protestant Missions and British Imperialism in the Nineteenth and Twentieth Centuries*, was one of the first works to argue that missionaries were not imperialists in the strictest sense of the

25. Sanneh, *Whose Religion is Christianity?* 22–24.

26. Yale-Edinburgh Group on World Christianity and the History of Christian Mission: http://divinity-adhoc.library.yale.edu/Yale-Edinburgh/.

27. Robert, "Naming 'World Christianity': Historical and Personal Perspectives on the Yale-Edinburgh Conference in World Christianity and Mission History," 1–18.

28. The field of World Christianity is the work of historians/church historians, theologians, sociologists, missiologists (those who study missions), statisticians, and anthropologists. While historians appear to be in the vanguard of the movement, the field remains highly collaborative. For a scholarly discussion, see Cabrita, *Relocating World Christianity* (2017).

meaning and that the relationship between missions and colonialism was marked by complexity.[29] In addition to his many scholarly monographs on World Christianity, Stanley has also served as the co-editor of the Studies in the History of Christian Mission (SHCM), a series of more than twenty-seven (to date) volumes that includes nearly 300 essays by academics on Christianity and missions in Latin America, Africa, and Asia.[30] In 2008, Liverpool Hope University established the Andrew F. Walls Centre for the Study of African and Asian Christianity in Liverpool, England.[31] The Centre, located in one of Britain's most famous port cities, was opened in Walls' honor to make room for the enlarging primary source materials becoming available for the study of non-Western Christianity.[32]

Barrett's research has continued under the auspices of an organization established in 2001 named the Center for the Study of Global Christianity, now situated on the campus of Gordon-Conwell Theological Seminary. The center's co-director, Todd Johnson, began working with Barrett in 1989, and collaborated with his colleague on several projects, including the 2001 edition of the *WEC*. Building on Barrett's groundbreaking work, the center launched the *World Christian Database* and the *World Religion Database*, the most sophisticated collections of electronic data on global religion.[33] The databases are now considered the most reliable sources of information on religion in the world[34] and are routinely cited by

29. Stanley, *The Bible and the Flag* (1992).

30. A complete listing of the volumes in this series, can be found at Eerdmans: https://www.eerdmans.com/Products/CategoryCenter.aspx?CategoryId=SE!SHCM.

31. Liverpool Hope University, Andrew F. Walls Centre for the Study of African and Asian Christianity: http://www.hope.ac.uk/andrewfwallscentre/.

32. "Andrew F. Walls Centre for the Study of African and Asian Christianity," 99.

33. *World Christian Database* (2004). The database is updated continually and available online at select universities and research centers. For subscription information, see https://www.worldchristiandatabase.org/.

34. See, for example, the evaluation of the Center's work by a team of Princeton scholars: Becky Hsu, "Estimating the Religious Composition of All

National Geographic, *The Economist*, and the *Wall Street Journal*. The sociologist Peter Berger said about the Center's work: "Ask them how many Lutherans there are in Mongolia, and how many Buddhists in Finland, they will within a few minutes come back with reasonably accurate numbers."[35] Gina Zurlo, the co-editor of the third edition of the *World Christianity Encyclopedia* (2020), also serves as the co-director of the Center for the Study of Global Christianity at Gordon-Conwell. While Zurlo is an early-career academic, she has already made significant contributions to the statistical and demographic study of World Christianity, and was named one of the BBC's 100 women of 2019.[36] Barrett and those who followed in his footsteps have given academics the ability to "count Christians" and advance research in World Religion and World Christianity.

This flurry of scholarly activity is not only transforming the way we think about the world, it is changing the way strategists think about world missions. One of Barrett's chief concerns in his research was to help the church give important consideration to the proper allocation of mission resources and foreign workers. His work was in many ways similar to James S. Dennis (1842–1914), the Princeton-educated missionary who a century earlier had made the study of statistics the handmaiden of mission strategy.[37] Although Barrett was a researcher, he remained a mission enthusiast, even serving as a consultant for mission organizations. The Southern Baptist Mission Board (SBMB), one of the largest mission agencies in the world, eulogized Barrett upon his death in 2011. The SBMB noted: "When David Barrett came to the foreign Mission Board as a consultant in 1985 less than 3 percent of our mission force was deployed to this last frontier [the unreached]. Today, as a result of Barrett's prophetic push, more than 80 percent of the people groups our missionaries serve are among the

---

Nations: An Empirical Assessment of the World Christian Database," 678–93.

35. "Celebrating 50 Years of Global Christian Research" (2015).

36. "Gina Zurlo ('17) Named as One of BBC's 100 Women of 2019," Boston University School of Theology.

37. Goodpasture, "Dennis, James Shephard," 176.

unreached."[38] In addition to his contributions in the fields of World Religion and World Christianity, Barrett's statistical work has altered the course of mission work by providing the world with an up-to-date census on the global distribution of religion, using a combination of globe trotting fieldwork and cutting-edge research powered by computer-generated technology.

Sanneh's work in the history of Christianity and missions has influenced other academics to widen their gaze, to consider the work of missionaries with greater openness, and to write about the new heartland of Christianity in the non-Western world. In 2001, Dana Robert, a colleague and friend of the late Sanneh, established the Center for Global Christianity and Mission at Boston University.[39] Robert, who did her doctoral work at Yale, has become a prolific writer in the field of World Christianity. Her prodigious research on the role of women as "gospel-bearers" shows (among other things) the central role women played in the rise of Christianity as a global faith.[40] Joel Carpenter, widely known for his work on American Christianity, turned his attention toward the global church later in his career.[41] In the early 2000s, Carpenter founded the Nagel Institute for the Study of World Christianity at Calvin College and has published numerous important works in the field of World Christianity. His research on the rise of Christian educational institutions in the non-Western world during the twentieth century has revealed both the vitality of non-Western Christianity as well as the challenges of creating sustainable models for education in the developing world.[42] The American historian Mark Noll (b. 1946), noted for his numerous works on eighteenth- and

38. "Mission Researcher David Barrett Dies," *Baptist Press*, August 8, 2011.

39. Boston University School of Theology, Center for the Study of Global Christianity and Mission: http://www.bu.edu/cgcm/about-us/history-of-the-center/.

40. Robert, *Gospel Bearers, Gender Barriers: Missionary Women in the Twentieth Century* (2002).

41. Joel A. Carpenter, Calvin College: https://calvin.edu/directory/people/joel-a-carpenter.

42. Carpenter, *Christian Higher Education: A Global Reconnaissance* (2014).

nineteenth-century American Evangelicalism, confessed that he was greatly influenced later in his career by developments in the global church.[43] Noll has made his own contributions to the field in works like *The New Shape of World Christianity: How American Experience Reflects Global Faith* and *Clouds of Christian Witnesses: Voices from Africa and Asia*. The British historian David W. Bebbington (b. 1949), widely known for his work on the history of politics and religion in Great Britain, as well as his definition of Evangelicalism (known as the "Bebbington Quadrilateral"), has broadened his scholarly labors to include global developments.[44] Bebbington's more recent works, like *Baptists through the Centuries: A History of a Global People* (2018) and *Victorian Religious Revivals: Culture and Piety in Local and Global Contexts* (2012), reflect the global expansion of Evangelicalism. He has also served as a doctoral mentor for scholars who are now teaching history and working in the field of World Christianity.[45] In recognition of Bebbington's immense contribution to the field of Evangelical studies, a new center is slated to open at Baylor University that will replace the Institute for the Study of American Evangelicals (closed in 2015) with one that encompasses the international character of Evangelicalism.[46] The University of Cambridge, the *alma mater* of Barrett, Stanley, and Bebbington, has also created a professorship in World Christianity, and the name of the Henry Martyn Centre has been changed to the Cambridge Centre for

43. Noll, *From Every Tribe and Nation: A Historian's Discovery of the Global Church* (2014).

44. For an introduction to the "quadrilateral," see Bebbington, *Evangelicalism in Modern Britain*, 1–19.

45. Bebbington and Larsen, *A Patterned Life: Faith, History and David Bebbington* (2014); Bebbington's works are too numerous to mention here. For a fairly comprehensive list that includes dissertations he has supervised, see Baylor University, Curriculum Vitae of David W. Bebbington: http://www.baylorisr.org/wp-content/uploads/Bebbington-CV-2018.pdf.

46. Baylor University, Evangelical Studies Program: https://www.baylorisr.org/programs-research/evangelical-studies/.

Christianity Worldwide to reflect the transformations occurring in the study of Christian history.[47]

Andrew Walls, David Barrett, and Lamin Sanneh were among the early pioneers in the field of World Christianity. At the beginning of the twenty-first century the writing of Christian history is being revised, buttressed by a sophisticated collection of statistics from researchers. The relationship between Christian missions and colonial expansion is being reconsidered, and new insights from history and statistics are being applied to contemporary missions. We now have a better understanding of how Christianity experienced this massive Southern shift during the twentieth century, and it is to this topic that we now turn.

47. Cabrita, *Relocating World Christainity*, 1–11.

3

Converting Colonialism

How Secular Critics of Missionaries Get It Mostly Wrong

"I go back to Africa to make an open path for commerce and Christianity; do you carry out that which I have begun. I leave it with you!"

—David Livingstone, 1857, Cambridge

IN BARBARA KINGSOLVER'S AWARD-WINNING novel *The Poisonwood Bible*, a Southern Baptist minister leaves Georgia in the "year of our Lord 1959" with his wife and four daughters. The Reverend Nathan Price was a sincere missionary, but his labors were hampered by obvious personal deficiencies. Price was largely disinterested in African culture and completely inept in the local language. He also had an irascible temperament. After more than a year of preaching without a single conversion, Price was beyond frustrated. As tensions mounted between the Southern Baptist missionary and the people of Kilanga, tribal elders decided to settle things the American way: "White men tell us: *Vote, Bantu*." The people decided this was a good way to implement the democratic ideals they had been taught by foreign missionaries. Two clay bows were set on the church altar—one for Jesus and the other against. The Reverend Price became visibly irate and tried to stop the "ridiculous" proceedings. Ignoring his remonstrations, the villagers dutifully lined up at the altar to exercise their right to vote. Following the election the assistant chiefs counted the pebbles and the results were announced. "Jesus Christ lost, eleven to fifty-six."[1]

It has become au courant in secular literature to portray missionaries as uncultured, arrogant, and largely ineffective. At times, missionaries are also pawned off as "employees" of the "religious department" of Machiavellian Western governments. It is interesting that Kingsolver cleverly weaves into her Poisonwood tale a secretive meeting of "a Belgian and an American" in Elisabethville (now Lubumbashi) to plan the 1961 assassination of Patrice Lumumba (1925–61).[2] (This piece of historical fiction is based on primary source materials that were released in 1975.) Her best-selling novel (which I rather enjoyed) leaves readers with the impression that the Reverend Price is unwittingly part of a grand conspiracy to exert Western control over the Belgian Congo by use of the combined forces of political intrigue and Evangelical zeal. Although her celebrated work contains grains of stereotypical truth, if Reverend Price is typical of Western missionaries, it is difficult to explain how the Congo became predominantly Christian during the second half of the twentieth century. If missionaries were merely pawns on the imperial chessboard, then why did the citizens of the Global South simultaneously reject colonial control while embracing the Christian message? As Philip Jenkins put it: "The runaway success of Christian missions to Africa and Asia are all the more striking in view of the extraordinary poor image that such activities possess in Western popular thought."[3]

The next two chapters explore the question of how Christianity experienced such rapid growth in the non-Western world during the twentieth century. It may appear self-evident to those who reject Kingsolver's caricature of twentieth-century missionaries

1. Kingsolver, *The Poisonwood Bible*, 327–34.

2. Kingsolver, *The Poisonwood Bible*, 317–24.

3. Jenkins, *The Next Christendom*, 39.

that the rapid expansion of Christianity in the non-Western world is primarily due to the successful efforts of Western workers. As we will see, this is indeed *one* of the causes. However, the researchers who have been working in dimly lit archives in some of the far-flung places where missionaries once toiled are telling a more interesting story. The study of World Christianity over the last fifty or more years by pioneers like Walls, Barrett, Sanneh, Stanley, Robert, and a growing company of highly trained academics has revealed that there are in fact multiple explanations for the growth of Christianity in the Global South. In this chapter, I focus on two of the causes of Christianity's exponential growth in the Southern Hemisphere, and briefly discuss how they are related to each other. The next chapter will be devoted to a third cause.

EUROPEAN EXPLORATION

European discovery is an important part of the story of the spread of Christianity to the non-Western world. American readers will remember the primary school rhyme: "In 1492 Columbus sailed the Ocean Blue." Recalling his arrival in the Bahamas on October 12, 1492, Columbus recorded his first act after stepping onto the shores of the New World: "To this island I gave the name San Salvador [Our Savior], in honor of our Blessed Lord."[4] Columbus was not a missionary; he was an Italian explorer whose expeditions had been bankrolled by the Catholic monarchs of Spain. But in the late fifteenth century the prevailing European worldview held that the discovery of new lands created opportunities for European monarchs not only to become rich but also to spread the riches of the gospel. Columbus promised the monarchs of Spain "as much gold as they may need" while in exchange they would also have the responsibility of "the turning of so many peoples to our holy faith."[5] It seemed a fair trade. The Spanish monarchs would take the gold, and in exchange the church would give the natives eternal

4. Columbus, *The Log of Christopher Columbus*, 75–76.

5. Columbus, *The Log of Christopher Columbus*, 200–201.

life. Thus began the tangled saga of the relationship between Christianity and Western colonial expansion in Latin America and much of the world.

During the early modern period (ca. 1500–1800) a growing number of European explorers set sail for the newly discovered lands of North America, Latin America, and the Caribbean Islands. Ambitious traders also wended their way along the coast of West Africa, then south around the Cape of Good Hope, then north again along the coast of East Africa, landing in places like Madagascar and Mombasa (Kenya). Using East Africa as a port, European ships struck out across the Indian Ocean to India and Indonesia and further away to New Guinea, Australia, New Zealand, and the Pacific Islands.[6] Ecclesiastics travelled with explorers, missionaries with merchants, clergy with convicts, and settlers with slaves, arriving at their destinations, often with different aims and purposes. It is far too simplistic, we now know, to assume that monarchs and missionaries and merchants all had the same motives, even if the missionaries and merchants boarded the same ships bankrolled by their monarch. It's a bit like saying that everyone on board a British Airways flight bound for Nairobi is a subject of the British Crown and travelling to Kenya on government business. However, Columbus and the explorers in his wake made it possible for the Christian message to spread to hitherto unknown regions of the world. It is fair to concede that Western colonial expansion aided in some way the spread of the gospel to the non-Western world.

The relationship between missionaries and monarchs was especially strong during the period from about 1492 to 1792, when there was no clear demarcation between faith and politics. Church and state were inextricably bound together even after the Protestant Reformation (ca. 1517–55), and the extension of political power to foreign soil often went hand-in-hand with the expansion of particular expressions of the faith. After 1648 and up to the American and French Revolutions, the Latin expression *cuius regio, eius religio* ("whose realm, his religion") was the law of the

6. Arnold, *The Age of Discovery* (2013).

land in Christian Europe.[7] If the king or queen was Catholic, then that was to become the religion of the land, as well as the new lands to which the sovereign might lay claim. This relationship between regents and religion had a long tradition in Latin America even before 1648, extending as far back as 1494, when Portugal and Spain divvied up large swaths of Latin America. (Protestant kings and queens largely ignored the treaties between Catholic monarchs.) The bishop of Rome (the pope) conferred authority upon Spanish and Portuguese monarchs to extend their kingdoms to newly discovered territories, a practice referred to as *patronato* in Spanish or *padroada* in Portugeuse. (These words are roughly translated into English as "privilege" or "power.") Catholic monarchs agreed to extend the kingdom of God to newly discovered lands after they had conquered indigenous people for the purpose of expanding their own kingdoms. Unfortunately, during the early modern period of imperial expansion, Western missionaries paradoxically carried the gospel of freedom to the very people their monarchs were also placing in subjection. The initial Christianization of Latin America by the Spanish and Portuguese was carried out by a militant form of Christianity, influenced to a large degree by the re-conquest of the Iberian Peninsula (Spain and Portugal). Soldiers became known as *conquistadores*—on a mission to "conquer" the land for king *and* Christianity. Even Franciscan missionaries like Diego de Landa Calderón (1524–79) were infamous for their harsh treatment of inhabitants who resisted conversion to the Catholic faith.[8] European expansion was marked by a particular machismo in Latin America.

Western monarchs also left their indelible impressions on Africa and Asia during the same period. The Portuguese built forts along the coasts of Africa, including the Gold Coast in Ghana, the Kongo (now Congo, at the mouth of the Zaire River), and Namibia. Chaplains and missionaries were frequently stationed on the coasts of newly discovered lands to minister to soldiers and baptize local inhabitants. In 1497 Vasco de Gama sailed around the Cape of

7. MacCulloch, *Christianity: The First Three Thousand Years*, 644.

8. González and González, *Christianity in Latin America*, 27–39.

Good Hope (South Africa) and in 1498 he made successive stops in Mozambique, Madagascar, Mombasa, and Malindi before continuing his voyage across the Indian Ocean for Calicut (Southwest India).[9] The famous Portuguese explorer set sail with missionaries and munitions, in search of souls as well as spices. On successive voyages the Portuguese established ports in Mozambique (Sofla) and modern-day Kenya (Mombasa), where in 1591 they built the famous Fort Jesus.[10] Western monarchs established beachheads in Goa (India), Malaysia, Vietnam, China, and Japan in the same century. Jesuit missionaries, arriving on Spanish ships in the Philippines in the late sixteenth century, spread the good news to the Philippine Islands, which remain predominantly Catholic to this day.[11] Monarchs, merchants, and missionaries became unlikely shipmates in the era of European exploration, making it difficulty to discern the distinction between Christianity and colonial expansion. When I visited Fort Jesus in Mombasa, Kenya many years ago and stood inside the magnificent stone edifice perched high above the waters of the Indian Ocean, I was reminded of how Jesus has often been associated with military power in places where missionaries have labored. The kingdoms of men and the kingdom of God were strange bedfellows during the era of European discovery. As Stephen Neill put it in 1964:

> Whether we like it or not it is the historic fact that the great expansion of Christianity coincided in time with the worldwide and explosive expansion of Europe that followed the Renaissance . . . .[12]

Christianity spread to Latin America, Africa, and Asia during the era of European discovery and colonization. This "historic fact" has sometimes made it difficult to distinguish between the expansion of Western colonies and the extension of the kingdom of God.

9. Moffett, *A History of Christianity in Asia*, 3.
10. Sundkler and Steed, *A History of the Church in Africa*, 45–72.
11. Tiedemann, "China and Its Neighbors," 369–86.
12. Neill, *A History of Christian Missions*, 414.

MISSIONARY ZEAL

Catholic and Protestant missionaries have played a vital role in the spread of the gospel to the Global South. The work of Catholic missionaries during the early modern period (ca. 1500–1800) was closely aligned with the state leading up to the Age of Revolutions (ca. 1775–1850). Throughout the sixteenth century, Roman Catholic missionaries from Portugal and Spain dominated the global evangelistic enterprise. As we have already observed, in sixteenth-century Latin America, missionaries were often closely aligned with the militant policies of Portugal and Spain, and local inhabitants were frequently press-ganged into the kingdom of God.[13] Abuses were commonplace, though it would be misleading not to mention that many outspoken clergy took umbrage with the mistreatment of local inhabitants. Antonio de Montesinos (1475–1514), whose effigy stands in Santo Domingo (Dominican Republic), famously rebuked his fellow countrymen in a public sermon during Advent, mounting the pulpit and declaring: "You are in mortal sin, and live and die therein, by reason of the cruelty and tyranny that you practice on these innocent people."[14] His bold example was an inspiration to Bartolomé de Las Casas (1484–1566), a Catholic cleric who spent most of his life lobbying against colonial abuses and calling for an end to the slave trade.[15] Although there were notable exceptions and heroic prophets, Catholic missionary endeavors in Latin American during the sixteenth century were complicit with imperial abuses.

Catholic missionaries also worked along the African coasts and in the distant lands of the Orient during the early modern period. On the African continent, wherever the Portuguese established forts, Catholic chaplains and Jesuit missionaries were actively engaged in evangelistic work. On occasions, priests reported baptisms that numbered into the thousands, though missionaries

13. González and González, *Christianity in Latin America*, 27–39.

14. Keen, *Latin America Civilization*, 71–72.

15. González and González, *Christianity in Latin America*, 30–33.

seldom ventured inland on the African continent before 1800.[16] Missionary work in Asia was marked by intense suffering as well as remarkable success during the early modern period. The Spanish missionary Francis Xavier (1506–52), one of the early leaders of the Society of Jesus (est. 1540) founded by the theologian and mystic Ignatius of Loyola (1491–1556), is renowned for his evangelistic successes. Xavier was an effective promoter of the gospel in India and Japan in the sixteenth century, and a notable advocate for contextualized witness. Jesuit missionaries who came after him lived to see the rise of a Christian century in Japan between 1550 and until about 1650, before it was stamped out by ghastly persecution.[17] During the seventeenth century, hundreds of Japanese Christians were slowly burned to death on stakes, while others were crucified on the beach in low water so they would slowly drown to death as the tide came in.[18] The brutal treatment of Christians in Japan in the seventeenth century is portrayed in Shusaku Endo's harrowing 1966 novel *Silence*, adapted for the screen and produced in 2016 by the award-winning film-maker Martin Scorsese (b. 1942).[19] Xavier's famous successor Mateo Ricci (1552–1610) entered China in 1583, and Christianity waxed and waned under successive emperors until persecution left the church in disarray by the end of the eighteenth century. The suppression of the Jesuits during the second half of the eighteenth largely quenched the flame of gospel witness in China.[20] While it is often difficult to distinguish between imperial expansion and evangelistic witness during the early modern period, some missionaries were critics of colonial abuses in Latin America, others were effective witness of the new faith along the coasts of Africa, and many missionaries to

16. Sundkler and Steed, *A History of the Church in Africa*, 42–64.

17. Moffett, *A History of Christianity in Asia*, 87–93.

18. Neill, *A History of Christian Missions*, 137.

19. McCracken, "Scorsese's 'Silence' Asks What It Really Costs to Follow Jesus: Martin Scorsese Adapts Shusaku Endo's Acclaimed Novel about Faith, Mission and Suffering," *Christianity Today*, December 16, 2016.

20. Moffett, *A History of Christianity in Asia*, 105–42.

Asia sacrificed their lives for the sake of the gospel and the people they came to serve.

Catholic missions entered a period of decline in the late 1700s just as Protestant missionary efforts began to flourish. The eighteenth century is sometimes referred to as the beginning of the modern missionary movement.[21] The modern missionary movement was greatly influenced by the rise of Evangelicalism, the creation of denominational and interdenominational mission societies, and an army of volunteers recruited from universities and Bible institutes. With the end of the Thirty Years' War (1618–48) in continental Europe, Protestant nations slowly began to turn their attention toward the wider world in order to spread the gospel message. Several important figures, all born in the early 1700s, spearheaded a movement that became known as Evangelicalism, a transatlantic phenomenon that was born out of the First Great Awakening (ca. 1730s–40s). The Methodist minister John Wesley (1703–91), the congregational pastor Jonathan Edwards (1703–58), and the Anglican cleric George Whitefield (1714–70) became early leaders of a transatlantic Protestant revival movement.[22] Wesley and Whitfield studied at Oxford together, and both had effective preaching ministries in England and New England. Edwards graduated from Yale, became a settled minister in New England, and produced a massive body of theological works that are still being edited by historians nearly 300 years later. Early Evangelicals were Protestants who emphasized the authority of the Bible (a Reformation trait), the centrality of the cross, the human need for conversion, and the responsibility of all Christians to actively bear witness to the gospel in word and deed.[23] Evangelicalism was not a denomination, but a diverse movement within the Protestant tradition comprising people from Anglican, Baptist, Congregational,

21. Neill, *A History of Christian Missions*, 204–9.

22. A very good introduction on Evangelicalism in the eighteenth century is Noll, *The Rise of Evangelicalism* (2003).

23. This definition of Evangelicalism has been followed by most academics working on the history of the movement since the 1990s. The classic work laying out this definition is found in Bebbington, *Evangelicalism in Modern Britain* (1989).

Methodist, Presbyterian, and other traditions on both sides of the Atlantic.[24] The word Evangelical (coined by Martin Luther) comes from a Latin word, *evangelicus*, that means pertaining to the gospel, signifying the great importance that Evangelicals place on understanding, applying, and proclaiming the claims of the gospel. Historian Douglas Sweeney helpfully defines Evangelicalism as "a movement of orthodox Protestants with an eighteenth-century twist."[25] Evangelicals are people who hold to the Christian orthodoxy of the Great Tradition and identify with many of the concerns of the Protestant Reformers. During the eighteenth century, they were Protestants who emphasized the need for people to be "born again" (conversion) in order to enter the kingdom of God. Due to the great stress Evangelicals have placed on the gospel and its implications, they have been especially engaged in the work of overseas missions. As Sweeney puts it so aptly, "Evangelicals care about nothing more than evangelizing the world."[26]

Jonathan Edwards may be best known for a sermon he preached in 1741 titled *Sinners in the Hands of an Angry God*, though this fiery discourse does not really communicate the New England minister's persona as a loving pastor and a "learned gentlemen" with a keen intellect.[27] Although Edward's public ministry and theological treatises contributed to the rise of the Evangelical movement, it was his publication of the diary of an otherwise obscure missionary to the Delaware Indians that would inspire Protestant missions during the modern period.[28] In 1749 Edwards published *An Account of the Life of the Late Reverend David Brainerd*. The work included a preface and introduction by Edwards, along with an edited version of Brainerd's personal diary recounting his trials and triumphs as a missionary in the New World.[29]

24. Noll, *The Rise of Evangelicalism*, 11–22.

25. Sweeney, *The American Evangelical Story*, 24.

26. Sweeney, *The American Evangelical Story*, 79.

27. Marsden, *Jonathan Edwards*, 214–26.

28. Conforti, "Jonathan Edwards' Most Popular Work: 'The Life of David Brainerd' and Nineteenth-Century Evangelical Culture," 188–201.

29. Minkema, "David Brainerd (1718–1747)," in Anderson, *Biographical Dictionary of Christian Missions*, 84–85.

Brainerd, who also attended Yale, was a family friend, and died at the age of twenty-nine under the care of the Edwards's family in their home in Northampton. Edwards, who had become the most famous minister in New England, was "ejected" from his pulpit the following year due to what he later called "misrepresentations" of his views by leading members of the congregation. Inspired by Brainerd's life, the well-known pastor retired from pubic view to serve as a missionary to the Mohican Indians in Stockbridge, assuming the presidency of the College of New Jersey (Now Princeton University) just before his death.[30] After Edward's passing, his life of Brainerd would live on, inspiring generations of Evangelicals to engage in the work of missions.

On the other side of the Atlantic, William Carey (1761–1834), a Baptist pastor from England, was deeply impressed by reading Edwards' life of Brainerd. In 1792 Carey penned a tract titled *An Enquiry into the Obligation of Christians to Use Means for the Conversion of the Heathens*.[31] Carey was a committed Evangelical pastor who was also enamored by the published accounts of the British explorer and cartographer Captain James Cook (1762–1805). A few months after penning his *Enquiry*, Carey preached a sermon to the leaders of the Northamptonshire Baptist Association in England in which he issued his now famous words, "Expect great things [from God]. Attempt great things [for God]."[32] In 1793 Carey was determined to lead the way for others by leaving his life as a settled pastor in England to serve as a missionary in British India. Carey's bold venture marked the beginning of a new era of missionary activity, wherein Protestants began forming societies and agencies as a means to send Christian workers to foreign fields. The Baptist Missionary Society (BMS), founded by Carey and Evangelical leaders in England in 1792, sent out missionaries to serve throughout the non-Western world in places like

30. Marsden, *Jonathan Edwards*, 375–94.

31. The 1892 edition of Carey's *Enquiry* was printed with a biographical introduction on Carey to commemorate the centennial of the Baptist Missionary Society he helped establish in 1792.

32. Carey, *An Enquiry*, xvii.

India, Ceylon (Sri Lanka), the West Indies (the Caribbean), China, Cameroon, the Belgian Congo, Angola, and Brazil.[33]

Carey's life and work set off a chain reaction in Britain and North America. Mission societies began appearing all over the Anglo-Atlantic world like modern-day franchises, producing thousands of foreign workers who boarded ships en route to the Southern Hemisphere to use every "means for the conversion of the heathen." The London Missionary Society, later to be associated with the Scottish missionary-explorer David Livingstone (1813–73), was established in 1795. In the following year came the Edinburgh Missionary Society (1796, renamed the Scottish Missionary Society in 1819) and the Glasgow Missionary Society (1796). The Church Missionary Society, a mission inspired by Anglican Evangelicals, was founded in 1799. In 1804, the British and Foreign Bible Society was created to promote cooperation between various denominations for printing and distributing the Bible throughout the world. Other societies from North America and Continental Europe were formed in the early 1800s: The American Board of Commissioners for Foreign Missions (1810), the Methodist Missionary Society (1813), the American Baptist Missionary Board (1814), the Basel Mission (1815), along with mission organizations in Denmark (1821), France (1822), Germany (1824), Sweden (1835), and Norway (1842).[34] While colonial expansion continued to aid Christian expansion in the modern period, missionaries were commissioned and supported, not by Western monarchs, but by churches, denominations, and mission societies.

During the nineteenth century, many Protestant missionaries were recruited from universities. The University of Cambridge was unusually influential in Protestant missions during the nineteenth century. Charles Simeon (1759–1836), who was educated at Eton[35]

33. Stanley, *The History of the Baptist Missionary Society*, 2.

34. Wolffe, *The Expansion of* Evangelicalism, 166–67; Neill, *A History of Christian Missions*, 251–52.

35. Eton is an independent boarding school for boys established in 1440 by King Edward IV. It is one of the most prestigious schools in the world, many of its students drawn from the British aristocracy. Most Eton graduates matriculate at Cambridge or Oxford.

and King's College, Cambridge, served as the Vicar of Holy Trinity Church and one of the founders of the aforementioned Church Missionary Society (1799).[36] Simeon was an Evangelical pastor who was known for his faithful expositions of Scripture, and his interest in foreign missions. During his tenure at Holy Trinity Simeon became friends with a young student named Henry Martyn (1781–1812). Martyn was a senior wrangler (first in his class in mathematics) at St John's, Cambridge. As a student he excelled in both mathematics and languages and upon completing his studies accepted a position as a Fellow at St John's. In 1802 Martyn read Jonathan Edward's life of David Brainerd and against the admonitions of his peers he immediately determined to give up his promising career as a Cambridge scholar to devote his life as a missionary to the Orient.[37] Martyn died in Iran from fever in 1812 at the age of thirty, though during his short career he produced Bible translations in Urdu, Arabic, and Persian. A trust was established in Cambridge in his memory and Henry Martyn Hall was built in 1887 next to Holy Trinity Church. The hall served as a library for mission studies and a gathering place for students who were interested in devoting their lives to Christian missions. The library established in Maryn's honor is now located at Westminster College and has been renamed the Cambridge Centre for Christianity Worldwide.[38]

The University of Cambridge was also the place where the missionary-explorer David Livingstone gave a speech in 1857 that would rouse a generation of missionaries. Standing in the Senate House with a beautifully illustrated map of central Africa as a backdrop, Livingstone spoke to members of one of the most

36. For the sake of American readers it may be helpful to note that the University of Cambridge, founded in 1209 AD, comprises thirty-one constituent self-governing colleges, along with a number of affiliated theological colleges and more than 100 academic departments and study centres.

37. Martyn, *Henry Martyn (1781–1812) Scholar and Missionary to India and Persia*, 15–20.

38. Papers related to the history of the Henry Martyn Hall, Minutes of the Meetings of the Trustees, Minute Book 1887–1939, HMH/2/1, archives of the Cambridge Centre of Christianity Worldwide (Cambridge, UK).

exclusive universities in the world. He gave a report on his recent exploits in Africa and concluded his speech with a plea for more missionaries:

> I beg to direct your attention to Africa;—I know that in a few years I shall be cut off in that country, which is now open; do not let it be shut again! I go back to Africa to make an open path for commerce and Christianity; do you carry out that which I have begun. I leave it with you![39]

A note describing the event reads: "The reception was so enthusiastic that literally there were volley after volley of cheers."[40] Livingstone's vision for Africa reverberated throughout the universities of Cambridge and Oxford, and leading members of the both universities immediately began working to establish another mission society. This society would encourage graduates from the leading universities in Britain to work as missionaries in central Africa. In 1858 the Oxford and Cambridge Mission to Central Africa was formed. It was subsequently renamed the Universities' Mission to Central Africa (UMCA) in order to accommodate recruits from other British universities who also wanted to give their lives to missionary service in Central Africa. Missionaries were drawn from distinguished graduates of the universities of Oxford, Cambridge, Dublin, and Durham, who worked to spread the gospel, eliminate the slave trade, establish medical clinics and hospitals, and set up schools and universities.[41]

A few years after the formation of the UMCA, the British Evangelical James Hudson Taylor (1804–88) established the China Inland Mission (CIM). He left Great Britain for China in 1866 with twenty-two volunteer missionaries who went out in faith, trusting God, rather than denominational support, to meet their needs. The CIM carried on in relative obscurity during the first twenty years

39. Livingstone, Speech "Delivered before the University of Cambridge, in the Senate-House, on Friday, 4th December 1857," 24.

40. Livingstone, Speech "Delivered before the University of Cambridge, in the Senate-House, on Friday, 4th December 1857," 24.

41. Wilson, *The History of the Universities' Mission to Central Africa*, 1–4.

of its existence until, in 1885, seven graduates of the University of Cambridge, referred to as The Cambridge Seven, volunteered to give up their lives of privilege to serve as overseas missionaries.[42] The American Evangelist D. L. Moody had given several addresses at both Oxford and Cambridge in 1882 and was himself greatly surprised by his own success. Moody had been invited to speak to student groups by the famous cricketer C. T. Studd (1860–1931), the leading member of The Cambridge Seven.[43] The American evangelist's sermons and the public testimonies of Cambridge students who had committed their lives to missions inspired a wave of university students to forego lives of privilege and volunteer to serve as missionaries in various parts of the world.[44] The Cambridge Seven put the CIM on the map of world missions while also inspiring the formation of other mission organizations like the Africa Inland Mission (AIM), one of the largest Protestant mission agencies in Africa.[45] Cambridge graduates continued to serve in overseas missions with distinction well into the twentieth century. The aforementioned Cambridge Centre for Christianity Worldwide (formerly the Henry Martyn Centre) contains a leather-bound gilt-edge book listing the names of a few of the many missionaries "who were formerly members of Cambridge Colleges who died in the service of Overseas Missions" between 1897 and 1941. Cambridge has arguably contributed more to the work of overseas missions than any university in the world.[46]

Not long after his evangelistic tour in Britain, D. L. Moody participated in a related missionary movement in the Untied States. Moody may be best known for his association with Moody Church (1864) in Chicago and his evangelistic globe trotting with

42. Pollock, *A Cambridge Movement*, 87.

43. For a popular account of Moody's addresses in Cambridge and Oxford, see Pollock, *A Cambridge Movement*, 54–88.

44. Pollock, *A Cambridge Movement*, 82–89.

45. Bacon, "From Faith to Faith: The Influence of the China Inland Mission on the Faith Missions Movement" (1983).

46. Barclay and Horn, *From Cambridge to the World* (2002); Randall, *The Cambridge Seventy* (2016); Randall, *Cambridge Students and Christianity Worldwide* (2019).

the singer and composer Ira D. Sankey (1840–1908), but his influence in world missions may be more significant than his work as either a pastor or an evangelist. In 1886 Moody established the Moody Bible Institute for the purpose of training laypersons for evangelistic work and overseas missions. Moody, though not university trained, had preached to students at Princeton, Oxford, and Cambridge. He was not opposed to recruiting university students for missionary service, but he believed that a much larger army was needed to carry out the work of global evangelism. He called his students "gap men" because he believed that even with professionally trained ministers and university-educated students toiling away in the world, there was still a great "gap" that could only be filled by laypersons. Moody's students were given a rudimentary education in Bible knowledge, then sent out to work in large urban cities in the United States and to serve as missionaries in Africa, Asia, and Latin America.[47]

The same year that Moody founded his Bible Institute he also presided over a conference for college students in Mount Hermon, Massachusetts with the mission enthusiast A. T. Pierson (1837–1911). It was at Mount Hermon that 100 students volunteered to become foreign missionaries and the Student Volunteer Movement (SVM) was born.[48] The SVM became a transatlantic Evangelical movement, recruiting students throughout North America and Europe. By 1891, at the First International Convention of the SVM, the number of volunteers for foreign work from North America alone stood at 6,200, with 321 having already sailed for the mission field.[49] When Hudson Taylor came to North America in 1888 to recruit missionaries for the CIM, he shared the platform with Moody at SVM gatherings and fanned the flames for young students to go out as missionaries with faith that God would provide their needs. A sense of excitement and urgency pervaded the 1880s and 1890s as young Evangelical students from

47. Brereton, *Training God's Army: The American Bible School*, 52–54.

48. Robert, *Occupy Until I Come*, vii.

49. Harder, "The Student Volunteer Movement for Foreign Missions and Its Contribution to 20th Century Missions," 143.

universities and Bible institutes poured into new and established societies adopting the watchword, "the evangelization of the world in this generation."[50] The missionary statesmen John R. Mott (1865–1955), who served with the YMCA and the SVM, popularized the watchword with the publication of his 1900 work bearing the movement's official slogan.[51] Already in 1900, Mott could boast: "The closing years of the nineteenth century have witnessed in all parts of Protestant Christendom an unprecedented development of missionary life and activity among young men and young women."[52] By 1902, nearly 2,000 missionaries had set sail from North America alone, and by 1910, the number had more than doubled to 4,336. By 1920, the numbered nearly doubled again to more than 8,140. The total number of young missionaries who went out to the field from the North American SVM movement was more than 13,000. When John Mott claimed that the majority of missionaries in the early twentieth century came from the SVM, he was hardly exaggerating.[53] People like Moody and Mott with international influence, lesser-known laypersons with Bible school diplomas, and graduates of prestigious universities who volunteered for "foreign" service were moved by a sense of evangelistic urgency to take the gospel to the non-Western world.

Missionary zeal did not diminish during the twentieth century. Even though Western Protestantism experience a schism during the Fundamentalist-Modernist Controversies (ca. 1910–40), endured a Great Depression (1929–39), which adversely affected missions funding, and battled the effects of two costly World Wars, volunteers who were committed to the missionary task remained calm, and carried on with the work of world evangelism.[54] Some Evangelicals saw in these tragic events the "signs of the times" evidenced by a growing apostasy of the last day as well as "wars

50. Robert, *Occupy until I Come*, 191.

51. Mott, *The Evangelization of the World in This Generation* (1900).

52. Mott, *The Evangelization of the World in This Generation*, 1.

53. Harder, "The Student Volunteer Movement for Foreign Missions and Its Contribution to 20th Century Missions," 144.

54. Treloar, *The Disruption of Evangelicalism* (2017).

and rumors of wars" that could mark the very end of the world.[55] Even several years after the Second World War, with the rising influence of communism in Africa and Asia during the Cold War (ca. 1945–90), Evangelicals warned that the world would soon be coming to an end. In 1951 the evangelist Billy Graham would say in his weekly radio address, "There are strong indications in the Bible that in the last days a great sinister anti-Christian movement will arise. At this moment it appears that communism has all the earmarks of this great anti-Christian movement."[56] Political developments, especially those of a menacing nature, steeled the resolve of Evangelicals in their commitment to carry the good news to foreign lands.[57] The historian of Christian missions Kenneth Scott Latourette (1884–1968) famously called the nineteenth century the Great Century for Christian missions, though the twentieth century would prove to be even greater. In the year 1900 there were 62,000 Christian missionaries working in foreign fields and by 1970, their number had nearly quadrupled to 240,000. During the thirty years between 1970 and 2000, when some were calling for missionaries to go home, the number of cross cultural missionaries nearly doubled, increasing to 420,000.[58] During the early modern period, Catholic missions were more closely associated with kings and queens, while during the modern period Protestant missions were largely inspired by Evangelical volunteerism.

"CONVERTING COLONIALISM"[59]

During the last fifty years, scholars have looked more closely at the relationship between Christianity, imperial expansion, and colonial rule. Due to the spread of Christianity by citizens of Western

55. Sutton, *American Apocalypse: A History of Modern Evangelicalism* (2014).

56. Graham, *Christianity vs. Communism* (1951).

57. Carpenter and Shenk, *Earthen Vessels: American Evangelicals and Foreign Missions, 1880–1990* (1990).

58. Zurlo, "World Christianity and Mission 2020." 17.

59. This phrase is taken from Robert, *Converting Colonialism,* 5.

nations it was sometimes assumed by historians that Christianity was an expression of imperial rule or even an agent of colonial expansion. This has turned out to be something of a *post hoc fallacy*—the faulty logic that "correlation implies causation." Even David Livingstone's words "commerce and Christianity" have been interpreted to mean that he was advocating the economic exploitation of Africans. It is true that during the modern colonial period subjects of the British crown in foreign lands sometimes considered missionaries and colonial administrators to be cut from the same cloth. There is a famous Kikuyu saying, "Gutiri mubia na muthungu" ("There is no difference between a missionary and a settler").[60] More jaundiced views went so far as to suggest that Western colonial powers used missionaries and the Christian message to exert control over their subjects. The Kenyan president Jomo Kenyatta (1897–1978) once famously quipped, "When the missionaries came to Africa they had the Bible and we had the land. They said 'Let us pray.' We closed our eyes. When we opened them we had the Bible and they had the land."[61] African politicians have often appealed to the history of colonialism to explain their national woes and win popular elections. Unfortunately, in retrospect, Western missionaries and mission societies often aligned themselves too closely with the policies and practice of their own governments. Many missionaries and mission agencies made uninformed and unwise decisions, and on too many occasions were blinded to their own mistakes. For example, the Africa Inland Mission (AIM), a very effective Evangelical faith-mission that placed a strong emphasis on evangelism over against the acquisition of land and the construction of buildings, was one of the largest landowners in the disputed region of Kenya's "White Highlands."[62] AIM missionaries even took pride in occupying and operating what it deemed to be the largest mission station in Africa during a period when land disputes were creating an all-out war in colonial

60. Cited in Hastings, *The Church in Africa*, 485.

61. Jomo Kenyatta, cited in Burton, *The Blessing of Africa*, 228.

62. Hastings, *The Church in Africa*, 424.

Kenya.[63] This is not to say that the mission intended to exploit the people it came to serve; it only bears witness to the foibles and failures of missionaries, who used the colonial apparatus for the purpose of carrying out their mission. It has become *de rigeur* for historians and novelists to tarnish the reputation of missionaries, taking delight in the ways in which they failed, only to miss one important and undeniable reality: missionaries were rather successful in spreading the gospel to the non-Western world, and non-Western people embraced Christianity even when colonial powers were told to go home![64]

Subsequent studies in the field of World Christianity have shown that Western missionaries during the modern period actually co-opted colonialism by making use of the opportunity it presented to travel the world and spread the good news. During the period of modern missions (beginning in the 1790s), missionaries more often than not "used" the colonial apparatus in order to carry out their work of evangelism, even at times opposing the policies of their own governments.[65] The relationship between missionaries and the governing authorities is characterized by complexity during the modern period, and explanations greatly depend on a variety of factors, including the period under consideration (before or after the Era of Revolutions), the convictions of individual missionaries, the policies of varied mission societies, and the different parts of the world in which missionaries served.[66] However, missionaries in general were more concerned with evangelism than imperialism.[67] Western workers stepped through the door that

63. Sandgren, *Christianity and the Kikuyu*, 30. Several works have been published on the Kijabe Mission Station and the Rift Valley Academy: Devitt, *On the Edge of the Rift Valley* (1992); Dow, *"School in the Clouds": The Rift Valley Academy Story* (2003); and Honer, *The Downing Legacy: Six Decades at Rift Valley Academy* (2010).

64. For a survey of how missionaries have been portrayed in literature and film, see Robert, *Christian Mission: How Christianity Became a World Religion*, 83–113 and Jenkins, *The Next Christendom*, 39–53.

65. Robert, *Converting Colonialism*, 5.

66. Porter, *Religion Versus Empire?* 316–30.

67. Stanley, *The Bible and the Flag* (2010).

was opened by European exploration and colonial expansion, sometimes bringing their Western baggage with them. But in the end they were very effective representatives of the kingdom of Christ.

Kingsolver's caricature of a failed Southern Baptist missionary is also misleading because of its male-dominated storyline. Young women who were often marginalized from positions of influence in Western societies found they were able to use their talents as doctors, teachers, preachers, linguists, and activists throughout the non-Western world.[68] Some of these female leaders became well known. Mary Lyon (1797–1849) was an early pioneer for women's education in the United States, and a promoter of Protestant overseas missions. She founded the Mount Holyoke Female Seminary (now Mount Holyoke College) in 1834 for the purpose of giving women equal access to education with the highest academic standards, inspiring female leaders to serve in every aspect of society, including overseas mission.[69] Perhaps the most famous Southern Baptist missionary during the modern period was Lottie Moon (1840–1912). She graduated from Virginia Female Seminary (now Hollins University) with a classical education, having mastered Latin, Greek, French, and Italian. (She would later become an expert in Chinese languages.) She served as a teacher and an evangelist in China until her death in 1912, and was an outspoken advocate of women's rights.[70] The Scottish Presbyterian Marry Slessor (1848–1915) served as a missionary to West Africa, opposed the widespread practice of infanticide, and became an effective advocate for the rights of women and children in southeast Nigeria.[71] Ida Scudder (1870–1960) was born to missionary parents in India, and graduated with a medical degree

68. Robert, "The Influence of American Missionary Women," 59–89.

69. Porterfield, *Mary Lyon and the Mount Holyoke Missionaries* (1979).

70. Neely, "Moon, Charlotte ('Lottie') Diggs (1840–1912)," in Anderson, *Biographical Dictionary of Christian Missions*, 471.

71. Hardage, *Mary Slessor, Everybody's Mother: The Era and Impact of a Victorian Missionary* (2008).

from Cornell in 1899. She served as a medical doctor in India, and in 1900 established the Christian Medical College in Tamil Nadu, now Vellore Hospital, one of the largest and most reputable research hospitals in the world.[72] The Albanian missionary Anjezë Gonxhe Bojaxhiu (1910–97), better known as Mother Theresa, founder of Missionaries of Charity (1950), may be the most celebrated missionary of the twentieth century.[73] While the work of female missionaries has been neglected in the scholarly literature, during the twentieth century an overwhelming majority of the world's missionaries, perhaps as many as two-thirds, were women.[74] As the *World Christian Encyclopedia* notes: "In short, there is no World Christianity to speak of without the contributions of women."[75]

I have spent significant time working in mission archives in North America, Europe, and Africa. I can tell you from personal experience that it is not difficult to find missionaries resembling the Reverend Nathan Price, Kingsolver's failed Southern Baptist missionary to the Belgian Congo. (That said, it is far easier to find abusive government officials!) However, her fictional character is atypical of the Christian missionary that left hearth and home to serve as an overseas missionary. Many missionaries were doctors, nurses, linguists, and teachers, most were better educated than their countrymen, and not a few were graduates of Ivy League[76] and Oxbridge (Oxford and Cambridge) universities.[77] Missionaries frequently opposed government abuses, worked to eradicate

72. Wilson, "Scudder, Ida Sophia," in Anderson, *Biographical Dictionary of Missions*, 609–10.

73. Spink, *Mother Theresa* (1997).

74. Robert, *American Women in Mission* (2005); Robert, *Gospel Bearers, Gender Barriers: Missionary Women in the Twentieth Century* (2002).

75. Johnson and Zurlo, *World Christian Encyclopedia* (2020), 27.

76. For examples of American missionaries who were educated at Ivy League institutions, see Putney and Burlin, *The Role of the American Board in the World: Bicentennial Reflections on the Organization's Missionary Work, 1810–2010* (2012).

77. For examples of missionaries educated at Cambridge, see Randall, *The Cambridge Seventy* (2016).

slavery, lobbied for better education, championed human rights, and with few exceptions, enjoyed and worked to preserve the cultures where they served. And the largest majority of missionaries during the modern period were not Southern Baptist men; they were women, from varied Christian traditions.[78] The fervent work of missionaries, men and women, changed the non-Western world during the twentieth century and contributed to rise of World Christianity. This is not a defense of the many flaws and foibles of Western Christian missionaries. However, Western missionaries were not first and foremost agents of Empire; they were fervent and effective witnesses of the gospel who "converted colonialism" to their own aims.[79]

There is, however, much more to the story of how Christianity became a world religion in the twentieth century.

78. For example, Woodberry, "Reclaiming the M-Word: The Legacy of Missions in Non-Western Societies," 3–12 and Robert, *Christian Mission: How Christianity Became a World Religion*, 83–113.

79. Robert, *Converting Colonialism*, 5.

4

The Surprising Work of God

Why the Work of Western Missionaries Is Only Part of the Story

"The wind of the Spirit is bringing new life and spiritual revival to Kikuyuland to-day. From other parts of Kenya, Tanganyika, Uganda, and Ruanda flashes the good news."

—Virginia Blakeslee, missionary in Kenya, 1950

On a cold winter day in Chicago our family boarded a flight bound for Nairobi where I would serve as a lecturer in church history at the Nairobi Evangelical Graduate School of Theology in Kenya (now, Africa International University). I had just finished my second postgraduate degree at one of the top divinity schools in the United States where my area of concentration was church history. I was excited to be in Africa with my family. We lived in a cottage "at the foot of the Ngong Hills" only a few miles from the farm of Karen Blixen (1885–1962), author of the 1937 memoir *Out of Africa*. Armed with an above-average pedigree with degrees in theology and church history and two decades of pastoral ministry experience, I felt confident in my ability to teach a survey course on the history of Christianity. Before the semester began I was privileged to spend time with Dr. Douglas Carew (1956–2012), the Vice Chancellor of the seminary. Doug (as he was known by faculty and friends) was a thoughtful, soft-spoken academic from Sierra Leone, and an influential leader in Evangelical circles in Africa. He was also a highly respected theologian and a contributor to the *African Bible Commentary*.[1] In the course of one of my early conversations with Doug we began talking about historical movements that had shaped the ethos of the church in East Africa during the twentieth century. I talked at length about how the theological background of many American and British Evangelical missionaries had (in my view) influenced African practices on ethics and morality. He listened intently until I finished my monologue and then responded in his usual fatherly manner: "I think you have made some interesting points. However, I would argue that the East African Revival had more to do with the nature of African Christianity in many parts of Kenya than the influence of Western missionaries." As he talked at length about a massive revival movement that I had never heard of, I realized then that my education in church history had only just begun.

If you know very little about some of the major global revivals that have happened (and are happening) in Africa, Asia, and Latin America—you are certainly not alone. I had an entire course on Jonathan Edwards (1703–58) and the "surprising work of God" of which he wrote in 1737. I had studied the writings of the American evangelist Charles Finney (1792–1875) and considered the global influence of the Second Great Awakening (ca. 1790–1840) and the Laymen's Prayer Revival (1857). I had learned about the effects of the Asuza Street Revival (1906) in North America, Northern Europe, and Latin America. I had studied the life and work of the American revivalist Billy Graham (1918–2018) and his influence on global Evangelicalism in the twentieth century. But it was not

1. Persuad, "Douglas Moses Carew, 1956–2012," *Dictionary of African Christian Biography.*

until I began teaching in Africa (and later undertook doctoral studies) that I began to realize that there were entire historical narratives on library shelves recounting the "surprising work of God" in the non-Western world. Some of these events (such as the East African Revival) have now been written about at length, though Western readers are only now beginning to learn about them.[2] This chapter provides an introduction to some of the massive revival movements of the twentieth century that have contributed to the rise of World Christianity. I have had to be intentionally selective, narrowing the focus to five of the largest revivals in the non-Western world. We have already observed that the Christian faith spread through European exploration as well as missionary zeal. However, indigenous revivals have also played a vital role in the expansion of Christianity in the non-Western world. In this chapter we will first turn our attention to Asia, the most populous continent on the planet and home to more than half of the world's 7.5 billion people, and cover three major revivals.

THE KOREAN REVIVAL OF 1906–7

The religious landscape of the Korean Peninsula was permanently altered during the twentieth century. Catholic missionaries began working in Korea as early as 1592, but sustained persecution, culminating in the death of 8,000–10,000 believers in 1866–67, severely weakened the Korean church.[3] Presbyterian and Methodist missionaries began arriving on the Korean peninsula in the 1880s and 1890s. In 1890, Samuel Austin Moffett (1864–1939), a Presbyterian missionary from Indiana, arrived in Korea with six other Presbyterian missionaries.[4] Moffett and his team adopted the principles of a mission strategist named John Livingston Nevius

2. For survey of some of the twentieth-century revivals that have contributed to significant transformations in the global church, see Shaw, *Global Awakening* (2010).

3. Moffett, *A History of Christianity in Asia*, 311–17.

4. Neely, "Samuel Austin Moffett (1864–1939)," Anderson, *Biographical Dictionary of Christian Missions*, 465.

(1829–93), a Princeton-educated missionary who had been working in neighboring China.[5] In 1896, Nevius published his work *Methods of Mission Work*, based largely on the lessons he had learned from his early failures and later successes as a missionary in China. He emphasized the importance of establishing a self-supporting and self-sustaining church at the very outset of missionary work. He also stressed the need for strong Bible teaching, the importance of engaging in evangelism without neglecting social responsibility, and he urged missionaries to provide quality education for church leaders. In addition, he worked to foster a spirit of unity between various Protestant missionaries working in Asia. These principles were followed and implemented by Presbyterian missionaries in Korea with surprising success. Between 1896 and 1900 the number of Christians in Korea increased from less than 5,000 to more than 20,000.[6] In an effort to equip church leaders to serve the rapidly growing church, Moffett founded the Presbyterian Theological Seminary in 1901 in the city of Pyongyang (now North Korea).[7] A revival soon broke out on the peninsula through indigenous witness, though transnational influences were also apparent.[8] One missionary shared reports of the Welsh Revival (1904–5) sweeping the British Isles, and local Korean churches began holding prayer gatherings, pleading for God to forgive their sins and bring renewal to the church.[9]

In 1906–7, late night gatherings were held throughout Korea, and church buildings were filled to capacity. A Presbyterian missionary working in Mopko, Korea wrote in 1906 that "the awakening in this place which began earlier in the year has grown steadily, until now there is not a square foot in the church."[10]

5. Hunt, "John Livingston Nevius," in Anderson, *Biographical Dictionary of Christian Missions*, 490.

6. Lee, *Born Again: Evangelicalism in Korea*, 13.

7. Neely, "Samuel Austin Moffett," 465.

8. For a summary of the revival including its transnational influences, see Kim and Kim, *A History of Korean Christianity*, 93–106.

9. Orr, *Evangelical Awakenings in Eastern Asia*, 27.

10. Preston, "The Awakening of Mopko," 32.

Another missionary wrote in the same year of "the remarkable awakening of the Korean people and the spirit of revival in many places."[11] Church members were gathering in the hundreds and thousands at meetings throughout the Korean peninsula, confessing their sins to God and each other, elders seeking forgiveness from ministers, ministers seeking forgiveness from one another, employees confessing sins to employers, all publicly mourning their transgressions. Some meetings lasted so late that missionaries were concerned about the physical well being of those attending and urged them to go home to rest, and if need be return the next day.[12] By 1907, church attendance in Korea had increased to over 100,000, nearly five times the 1900 figure.[13] A January 1908 report reflecting on the previous year compared the revival to the book of Acts: "The story of the great progress of modern missions in Korea reads like the story of the gospel in apostolic days."[14]

The effects of the revival continued after 1908, with numerous men and women also deciding to devote their lives to the vocational ministry. In 1912, church membership in Korea totaled over 300,000 in a nation of 12 million people.[15] Even after the peninsula was divided into North Korea and South Korea in 1948, the long effects of the Korean Revival remained visibly evident. Thousands of Christians migrated from North Korea to South Korea in order to escape persecution, though a tiny catacomb church remained (and remains) in the hermit kingdom of the north.[16] In the wake of the Korean Revival, Christianity in South Korea continued to grow unabated in the second half of the twentieth century. Even Pentecostal churches, first established in Korea in the late 1940s, have a distinct Presbyterian flavor due to the prolonged influence

11. Chester, "Church Union in Kenya," 23.

12. Koch, *Victory Through Persecution*, 16–17.

13. Lee, *Born Again: Evangelicalism in Korea*, 13.

14. "Korea," *The Missionary*, 36.

15. Koch, *Victory Through Persecution*, 29.

16. Koch, *Victory Through Persecution*, 26–27; On the status of Christianity in North Korea, see Johnson and Zurlo, *World Christian Encyclopedia* (2020), 598–601.

of the Korean Pentecost of 1906–7.[17] South Korea is now home to the largest Presbyterian church in the world, with a reported weekly attendance of 100,000 people. The world's largest megachurch church, referred to earlier, can also be found on the Korean peninsula, with Sunday attendances that are reported at 800,000.[18] While Western missionaries have played a part in the growth of Christianity in Korea, their role has been modest. Korean Christianity has largely grown through national revival and indigenous witness.

THE DORNAKAL REVIVAL IN INDIA

A massive movement of new converts entered the church in India during the 1920s and 1930s that has contributed to a sizeable presence of Christians in a nation of 1.4 billion people. The epicenter of the revival was located in Dornakal and its outlying villages to the south and east of the city of Hyderbad.[19] The movement has therefore been dubbed the Dornakal Revival.[20] The leader of the movement was V. S. Azariah (1869–1948), the son of an Anglican priest, who began his evangelistic ministry in 1895.[21] While studying at Madras Christian College (est. 1837), Azariah began working for the YMCA, and became friends with the American missionary-evangelist George Sherwood Eddy (1871–1963) and the mission enthusiast John R. Mott (1865–1955). Azariah worked for the YMCA from 1895 to 1909, during which time he engaged in itinerating evangelistic work and helped establish the Indian Missionary Society (1903) and the National Missionary Society (1905). In 1909, Azariah moved with his family to Dornakal believing he was called to work as a missionary among the depressed

17. Anderson, *An Introduction to Pentecostalism*, 1–4.

18. Bird, "The World's Largest Churches," *Leadership Network.*

19. Orr, *Evangelical Awakenings in Southern Asia*, 107–43.

20. Shaw, *Global Awakenings*, 67–90.

21. Harper, "Azariah, Samuel Vedanayagam," in Anderson, *Biographical Dictionary of Christian Missions*, 35–36.

classes.[22] He opened his ministry center in an abandoned brewery and after only three years of effective evangelist work he had gained such widespread notice that he was ordained as the first Indian bishop in the Anglican Church.[23] He devoted the larger part of his ministry to the lower castes, teaching India's "outcasts" that they were loved and accepted by God, and endowed with dignity by their Creator.[24] He was a strong advocate of indigenous church leadership and lay evangelism, requiring new converts to place their hands on their heads at baptism and say, "Woe unto me if I preach not the gospel."[25] He believed that Christianity should embrace local expressions of Indian culture, and he encouraged the faithful to enjoy Indian food, drink, fashion, and music. He even adopted South Asian architectural styles in the design of the cathedral church in Dornakal, making use of the onion (or bulbous) domes to make a statement about Christ's love for Indian culture. Between 1921 and 1931, an average of 12,085 converts were being baptized *every month* in South India, adding more than 1.4 million members to the church in a single decade. The churches in Azariah's diocese grew most rapidly, and even during the decade of the 1930s as growth began to slow, the Dornakal church was growing at a rate of more than 11,500 new converts a year.[26] The mass movement of the poor entering the church attracted the attention of Mahatma Gandhi (1869–1948) who expressed concern that Azariah's evangelistic work might further entrench the lower classes in the colonial apparatus and thereby undermine his own efforts to unite the Hindu people of India.[27] Gandhi was wrong. In 1947, India gained its independence, and Congress, with the support of Hindu legislators, voted to protect freedom of religion,

22. Harper, *In the Shadow of the Mahatma*, 96.

23. Harper, *In the Shadow of the Mahatma*, 96.

24. Harper, *In the Shadow of the Mahatma*, 190.

25. Harper, *In the Shadow of the Mahatma*, 193.

26. Statistics are drawn from the *Dornakal Diocesan Magazine* from the period 1928–41 and can be found in Harper, *In the Shadow of the Mahatma*, 185, fn. 25.

27. Harper, *In the Shadow of the Mahatma*, 291–351.

including the Christian minority who were advocates of Indian independence.[28] More recent studies now point to the growth of Evangelical Christianity and the revival in South India as important contributors to the rise of India as an independent nation.[29] Indian Christians are proud of their national identity and supporters of the free exercise of all religions, though they have sometimes been victims of persecution in their own country.[30] Western missionaries have served with distinction in India, though it is estimated that indigenous witness is responsible for 85 percent of conversions to Christianity in one of the most diverse regions of the world.[31]

THE INDONESIAN REVIVAL

The church in Indonesia experienced a great awakening between 1965 and 1971, and has continued to grow steadily in the world's most populous Muslim nation.[32] Indonesia is comprised of some 13,000 islands (6,000 of them inhabited) stretching across the equator and occupying an area that is nearly three times the size of the state of Texas.[33] Inspired by the beauty of what was then occupied by the Netherlands, a nineteenth-century Dutch poet referred to Indonesia as "a girdle of emerald flung around the equator."[34] In 1900, there were some 536,000 Catholic and Protestant

28. Bauman and Ponniah, "Christianity and Freedom in India," in Hertzke and Shah, *Christianity and Freedom*, 222–53.

29. Aaron, "Emulating Azariah: Evangelicals and Social Change in the Dangs," 87–130.

30. For a recent study by a major academic press see Bauman, *Pentecostals, Proselytization, and Anti-Christian Violence in Contemporary India* (2015).

31. Frykenberg, *Christianity in India*, 1–20.

32. I am indebted to Brian Stanley for first introducing me to the global phenomenon of vibrant Christian communities in Islamic nations. See Stanley, "Aliens in a Strange Land? Living in an Islamic Context in Egypt and Indonesia," 173–92.

33. "Indonesia—Location, Size, and Extent," *Nations Encyclopedia*.

34. Wintle, *An Economic and Social History of the Netherlands, 1800–1920*, 216.

Christians scattered throughout Indonesia, comprising 1.4 percent of the population.[35] Between 1936 and 1939, the well-known Chinese evangelist John Sung (1901–44), known for his conservative Evangelical convictions and his verse-by-verse expositions of Scripture, held evangelistic tours in Indonesia with remarkable success.[36] One of the important results of Sung's peripatetic labors and earnest Bible expositions (an unusual style for evangelists) was the establishment of new churches marked by Evangelical traits.[37] The church in Indonesia experienced moderate growth in the 1940s through the 1950s, and accelerated rapidly in the 1960s when a momentous revival erupted on the volcanic archipelago.

Biographers of the revival have suggested numerous possible causes for the awakening, but political developments were pivotal.[38] After gaining its independence in 1945, the former Dutch stronghold felt the direct effects of the Cold War. In 1965, Indonesian communists attempted a military coup. The rebellion was brutally quashed in one of the least publicized, and most horrific mass killings in the twentieth century. Approximately 500,000 Indonesians were brutally tortured and murdered by their own countrymen in a government-sponsored backlash intended to stamp out communist opposition. Some estimates place the number of dead closer to 1 million.[39] In 2015, an independent enquiry held the Indonesian government responsible for the atrocities, though evidence was uncovered that British, Australian, and American intelligence agencies were also complicit in the crimes.[40] The political maelstrom was the backcloth for one of the largest revivals of the twentieth century. A 1967 article in *Life Magazine* reported that

35. "Indonesia," in Barrett, *World Christian Encyclopedia*, 372.

36. Lyall, *John Sung*, 178.

37. Aritonang and Steenbrink, *A History of Christianity in Indonesia*, 42–64.

38. The most reliable study of the revival is found in Willis, *Indonesian Revival* (1977).

39. Smail, "Descent into Chaos," 335–37.

40. Santoso and Klinken, "Genocide Finally Enters Public Discourse," 594–608.

the "church leaders of Indonesia agree that the greatest impetus came when an attempted Communist coup was overthrown in September 1965."[41] A study published in 1977 found that converts cited political unrest in the nation as the primary influence in their decision to turn to the church for spiritual sustenance and moral guidance.[42] While various secondary causes have been suggested by biographers of the revival (some, likely legendary), there is widespread agreement that a significant stimulus came from student-led evangelistic teams sent out to neighboring islands from the Indonesian Gospel Institute in East Java during the summers of 1965–66.[43] New converts also credited the response of the Indonesian church to the mass killings as an important factor in their conversion decision. Christians refused to participate in the murder of their communist neighbors, issued public calls for peace, and actively shared their faith with fellow citizens, even providing pastoral care for those in prison who were being held as communist sympathizers.[44]

The church throughout the islands of Indonesia experienced unprecedented growth between 1965 and 1971. In November 1967, *Christian Life* reported that Indonesia "is in the midst of what may be the greatest revival of the twentieth century."[45] The following month *Christianity Today* informed its readers that "Indonesians are turning to Christianity on a scale unprecedented in modern times anywhere in the world," reporting that some 400,000 converts had been baptized over the previous two years. The same article noted that the church was growing with such rapidity that the Muslim community had begun to worry that Christianity might actually take over the nation.[46] The revival

41. "Islands See Miracles," *Christian Life* (November 1967), 23.

42. Willis, *Indonesian Revival*, 18.

43. Wiyono, "Timor Revival," 269–93; Aritonang and Steenbrink, *A History of Christianity in Indonesia*, 875.

44. Willis, *Indonesian Revival*, 18.

45. "Islands See Miracles," *Christian Life* (November 1967), 22–23.

46. "Indonesia: Turmoil amid Revival," *Christianity Today* (December 22, 1967), 40.

cut across denominational, ethnic, and geographical boundaries, and was especially strong in East and Central Java, Northern Sumatra, Borneo, and Timor.[47] Miraculous healings, outbreaks of *glossolalia*, physical resurrections, and other sensational phenomenon were recounted by revival participants, though some reports were likely sensationalized.[48] What is not in dispute is the massive number of recorded conversions and baptisms. Between 1965 and 1971, more than 2 million people were added to the Indonesian church, primarily within Evangelical congregations.[49] During the same period, the United Bible Society (UBS) reported that Scripture distribution increased from 182,000 to more than 3 million![50] Between 1900 and 1970, the church in Indonesia grew from 558,000 adherents, or 1.4 percent of the population, to more than 11.2 million, comprising nearly 10 percent of the population of Indonesia.[51] By the mid-1990s, the size of the church more than doubled to more 25 million adherents, about 12 percent of the population, with the growth of the church continuing unabated into the early twenty-first century.[52] Some regions of Indonesia, such as Nusa, Tenggara, Timor (in the Lesser Sunda Islands), and Irian Jaya (West Papau) are now predominantly Christian. Timor is now 90 percent Christian, while nearly 70 percent of the people of Irian Jaya claim to be followers of Christ. As already observed, mega churches are not uncommon in Indonesia, with numerous congregations reporting weekly attendances above 10,000 and

47. Willis, *Indonesian Revival*, 12.

48. The sensational reports were discussed in Plowman, "Demythologizing Indonesia's Revival," *Christianity Today* (March 2, 1973), 49–50. The miracles were defended in Koch, *Wine of God: Revival in Indonesia, Formosa, Solomon Islands, and South India* (1974).

49. Aritonang and Steenbrink, *A History of Christianity in Indonesia*, 870; Willis, *Indonesian Revival*, xiii.

50. Willis, *Indonesian Revival*, 16.

51. Johnson and Zurlo, "Indonesia," in *World Christian Encyclopedia* (2020), 394.

52. Johnson and Zurlo, "Indonesia," in *World Christian Encyclopedia* (2020), 394.

several reporting attendances larger than 30,000.[53] One cannot help but recall the words of Isaiah the prophet, "Let them give glory to the LORD and proclaim his praise in the islands."[54] Christianity is flourishing in a nation that is predominately Muslim and spreading through the effective witness of Indonesian Christians who are actively sharing their faith.

THE EAST AFRICAN REVIVAL

On the African continent revival swept through the region of Ruanda-Urundi (now Rwanda and Burundi, Southwest of Lake Victoria), Uganda, Kenya, and Tanganyika (now Tanzania) during the 1930s and 1940s. The East Africa(n) Revival was spearheaded by the Cambridge-educated medical missionary John E. ("Joe") Church (1899–1989) and the Ugandan evangelist Simeon Nsibambi (1897–1978), who was educated in Anglican mission schools. The movement transformed the church in East Africa, and its effects were so remarkable that they remain visibly evident in the early twenty-first century. The history of the massive revival has been preserved due in large measure to the John Edward Church Papers (JECP), a large collection of primary sources housed at the Cambridge Centre for Christianity Worldwide. "Joe" Church and Simeon Nsibambi were concerned about what they perceived to be a liberal drift within the mission-established Anglican Church in the late 1920s after a period of significant church growth in Uganda that had begun thirty years earlier.[55] Church and Nsibambi became close friends, African evangelist and British missionary travelling together, eating together, praying together, preaching together, and working as equal partners in the gospel. In their preaching they stressed the importance of genuine conversion, a strong Evangelical theme that soon gave the movement another name—the

53. Bird, "The World's Largest Churches," *Leadership Network.*

54. Isa 42:12.

55. MacMaster, *A Gentle Wind of God: The Influence of the East Africa Revival*, 30–31.

Balokole, a Luganda word that means "saved ones."[56] They confronted clerical complacency (among Africans and missionaries), boldly called for racial reconciliation, emphasized the equality of male and female, and urged people to work together for renewal within the church. Their message was often attended with the public confession of sins, pastor and people openly seeking forgiveness from God and each other, accompanied at times with all night prayer and singing.[57] The movement spread rapidly through small groups, revival fellowships, crowded conventions, and travelling evangelistic teams. From small beginnings in Ruanda and Burundi (then the Belgian territory of Ruanda-Urundi) and Uganda, the revival crossed into Western Tanzania (then Tanganyika) and by the late 1930s and early 1940s it was spreading throughout Kenya. The Kenya novelist Ngũgĩ wa Thiong'o recalled the 1940s when "the revivalist movement reached Kenya and swept through the ridges like a fire of vengeance."[58] The surprising work of God began within the Anglican community, but it soon spread to other denominations, including the Africa Inland Mission (which formed the Africa Inland Church in 1943), Mennonites, Methodists, and Presbyterian, and also influenced Roman Catholics.[59] Not a few missionaries, along with some Africans, opposed the movement due to the controversial practice of publicly confessing "embarrassing" sins as well as the challenge that some revivalists created for mission authority. Some missionaries expressed concerns over some of the progressive social changes that pro-revivalists advocated. For example, a few members of the Africa Inland Mission (AIM) complained about the "erroneous doctrine" of the revival, which they specified as the "confession of sin, mostly in connection with sex, and an attempt to break down all restraining bars

56. Ward and Wild-Wood, *The East African Revival*, 18–20.

57. Church, *Quest for the Highest*, 131.

58. Thiong'o, *A Grain of Wheat*, 82.

59. Githii, *The East African Revival Movement and the Presbyterian Church of East Africa*, (1992); Wanyoike, *An African Pastor*, 151–73; MacMaster, *Gentle Wind of God*, 67–79.

between colour, race, and sex."[60] Some missionaries were calling for things to be done "decently and in orderly" in worship services (a sound biblical policy), while at the same time tolerating segregation and sexism.[61] Most missionaries, even many AIM missionaries, sided with the pro-revivalists, giving praise to God that "In Him there is no black and white, but all one" and rejoiced that "the wind of the Spirit is bringing new life and spiritual revival to Kikuyuland to-day" as well as "Tanganyika, Uganda, and Ruanda."[62] Many Western missionaries were so influenced by the revival during the 1940s and 1950s that upon returning to Europe and North America their stories inspired renewal movements in their sending churches and denominations.[63]

The influence of the East African Revival endured throughout the second half of the twentieth century, and the effects of the movement were in effect institutionalized through the East African Revival Fellowship (or Revival Brethren), the circulation of periodicals like *Revival News* and "Joe" Church's own account of the revival published in 1981.[64] In the year 1900, there were a mere 200 Christians in the region of Ruanda-Burundi (Rwanda and Burundi after 1962) and by 1970 there were nearly 5 million Christians in the region where the revival had begun some forty years earlier. By 1990, the number of Christians doubled to more than 10 million, with more than 80 percent of people in both countries identifying with the Christian faith.[65] In Uganda, the number of Christians increased from 180,000 in 1900, to more than 14 million in 1990,

60. Africa Inland Mission, Kenya Field Council Minutes, December 6–10, 1948, Richard Gehman Papers, Billy Graham Center Archives (Wheaton).

61. Peterson, *Ethnic Patriotism and the East Africa Revival*, 211–14.

62. Margaret Lloyd, "Echoes of Revival," 57; H. Virginia Blakeslee, "Revival News," 44.

63. MacMaster, *A Gentle Wind of God*, 119–61.

64. Church, *Quest for the Highest* (1981). The various newsletters of the movement are housed at the Cambridge Centre for Christianity Worldwide in the John Edward Church Papers, See also Peterson, *Ethnic Patriotism and the East African Revival*, 47.

65 Barrett, *World Christian Encyclopedia* (2001), 160, 629.

representing 87 percent of the population.[66] The number of Christians in Kenya stood at 5,000 in the year 1900, increasing to 7.2 million in 1979, and 18.4 million by 1990. Christianity in Tanzania also experienced a marked increase during the same period, from 92,000 Christians in 1900 to more than 12.2 million in 1990.[67]

It is difficult to assess the degree to which any revival directly contributes to the growth of the church in a particular region, however the effects of the East African Revival were widespread and enduring. A 1973 study spearheaded by David Barrett estimated that in Kenya "over ninety per cent of all clergy in the Anglican, Presbyterian and Methodist churches, including the whole of their national leadership, belong to the Revival Fellowship."[68] In 2013, the Global Anglican Future Conference (GAFCON), which now represents the largest body of Anglicans in the world, held their international gathering in Nairobi, Kenya. GAFCON drafted and adopted the Nairobi Communiqué and Commitment, invoking the East African Revival as the continued inspiration for its commitment to the authority of Scripture, the centrality of the gospel, as well as its traditional views on marriage and human sexuality.[69] The Anglican tradition has been greatly influenced by twentieth-century revival, and it is growing more African as well as flourishing numerically.[70] In 2016, the esteemed moderator of the Presbyterian Church of East Africa, John Gatũ (1925–2017), singled out the "East African Revival Fellowship" that he had been a member of since his conversion (ca. 1935) as one of the greatest influences in his life. The Revival quickened the numerical growth of the African church, broke down racial barriers between

66 Barrett, *World Christian Encyclopedia* (2001), 763.

67 Barrett, *World Christian Encyclopedia* (2001), 729.

68. Barrett, *Kenya Churches Handbook*, 117.

69. "Nairobi Communiqué and Commitment," October 26, 2013.

70. Niebuhr, "As the Old-Line Anglican Churches Wilt, Those in Africa Flower Profusely," *New York Times*, August 2, 1998; "US Anglicans Join Kenyan Church," *BBC News*, 30 August 2017.

missionaries and Africans, and contributed to the Evangelical ethos of contemporary global Christianity.[71]

THE BRAZILIAN PENTECOST

In Latin America, a Brazilian Pentecost has been underway since the 1970s and researchers have now turned their attention South to understand the causes of one of the most dynamic movements in World Christianity.[72] Between 1900 and 1960 more than 90 percent of Latin Americans identified with Roman Catholicism, the faith of the sixteenth-century conquistadores. A seismic shift in the religious landscape has taken place as tens of millions of Latinos have become Evangélicos (Protestants), more than half of which self identify as Pentecostal.[73] In Brazil, the growth of Pentecostalism has become palpable, with more than 70 percent of Evangélicos indicating that they are Pentecostal.[74] After the Azusa Street Revival in Los Angeles (1906), Pentecostal missionaries fanned out in the spirit of Acts 2 for the purpose of spreading the revival movement to the ends of the earth.[75] In 1910, Luis Francescon (1866–1964), an Italian immigrant from Chicago who had been influenced by Azusa Street, arrived in Sao Paulo, Brazil, where he planted the *Congregazione Cristiana* (CC, Christian Congregations) in a large Italian community in the city. In the same year, two Swedish Baptists, Gunnar Vingren (1879–1933) from Chicago and Daniel Berg (1884–1963) from South Bend, Indiana, left for Belém, Brazil and established the Apostolic Faith Mission, later named Assembléia de Deus (AD, Assembly of

71. The majority of the world's Christians hold to traditional views on Scripture, marriage, and human sexuality. Jenkins, *The New Faces of Christianity: Believing the Bible in the Global South* (2006).

72. Freston, "Contours of Latin American Pentecostalism," 221–24.

73. Bell, "Religion in Latin America: Widespread Change in a Historically Catholic Region," *Pew Research Center*, November 13, 2014.

74. Shaw, *Global Awakening*, 137.

75. Anderson, *To the Ends of the Earth: Pentecostalism and the Transformation of World Christianity*, 43–50.

God). While independent (non-Pentecostal) faith missions had been working in Brazil since the late nineteenth century, they had garnered very little following due in part to their unwillingness to relinquish control to indigenous leaders.[76] In contrast, Pentecostal missionaries from North America and Europe adopted a policy of local empowerment at the very outset of their work. As a direct result of this policy of empowerment, from the 1910s through the 1950s, Pentecostalism in Latin America became more indigenous and increasingly diverse.[77] Pentecostalism is not bound together by a common creed, or uniform liturgy, or unifying hierarchy. The movement is therefore prone to schism. Paradoxically, the fissiparous nature of Pentecostalism has contributed to its growth, as spin-off churches and denominations have spread throughout the nation with a degree of "social flexibility" that does not require adherence to a fixed institutional standard.[78]

Beginning in the 1970s, the indigenous Pentecostal church in Brazil experienced rapid growth as entrepreneurial pastors harnessed modern technology and created mass appeal with populist preaching styles, rhythmic worship experiences, and a gospel that promises a better life for believers on earth as well as in heaven.[79] For example, the Universal Church of the Kingdom of God (Universal Church) in Sao Paulo, founded by Edir Macedo in 1977, now claims to have more than 2 million members worldwide, with a network of congregations in more than 200 countries and territories around the world. In 2014, the church built a magnificent auditorium that seats 10,000 worshippers. The building is designed after the ancient temple in Jerusalem, fittingly named the Temple of Solomon.[80] This ostentatious display of wealth may seem out of

76. Chestnut, *Born Again in Brazil*, 30.

77. Shaw, *Global Awakening*, 137–40.

78. Freston, "'Neo-Pentecostalism' in Brazil: Problems of Definition and the Struggle for Hegemony," 147.

79. David Masci, "Why Has Pentecostalism Grown So Dramatically in Latin America?" *Pew Research Center*, November 14, 2014.

80. "Pentecostalism in Brazil: From Modesty to Ostentation," *The Economist*, January 23, 2016.

place in a city so rife with poverty, but this is precisely one of the appeals of modern Pentecostalism. Just as the villagers of ancient Palestine found encouragement in God's promises of reward with their gazes transfixed on the beauty of Solomon's temple, those who dwell in Brazilian favelas have found in Pentecostalism a message of hope that their lives can somehow become better here and now.[81] This controversial message, often referred to as the "prosperity gospel," has roots in some of America's most influential mega-churches and has found a home in Brazilian Pentecostalism.[82] Prosperity theology is pervasive in Latin America, with a majority of all Protestants in Brazil affirming their belief in the statement that "God will grant wealth and good health to believers who have enough faith."[83] The desire for health and wealth, especially among the poor in Latin America, is one of the reasons for the growth of Pentecostalism in Brazil.[84] However, reductionism should be avoided in interpreting the cause of Pentecostalism's growth solely on the basis of the promises of the prosperity gospel. A 2014 study published by the *Pew Research Center* indicated that Brazilians indicated that their number one reason for converting to Protestantism was that it aided them in cultivating a personal relationship with God (77 percent). The survey also revealed that Evangélicos preferred the style of worship (68 percent), the emphasis on personal morality (61 percent), and ranked the church's promise of a better financial future near the bottom (21 percent). While the reasons for the Brazilian Pentecost continue to be debated, no

81. Bailey, "How the Prosperity Gospel is Sparking a Major Change in Predominantly Catholic Brazil," *The Washington Post*, October 31, 2017.

82. The best scholarly introduction to the history of the prosperity gospel in America is Bowler, *Blessed: A History of the American Prosperity Gospel* (2013); Also see Brouwer, *Exporting the American Gospel*, 20–28. While I do have some significant disagreements with the broad definition of "global Fundamentalism" in this work, the study effectively argues that many American religious ideas, such as the prosperity gospel, have been exported to the non-Western world.

83. "Religion in Latin America: Pentecostalism," *Pew Research Center*, November 13, 2014.

84 This is the central argument made in Chestnut, *Born Again in Brazil* (1997).

one disputes that a religious revival has increased the number of Christians in Brazil from 17 million in 1900, to nearly 160 million in the year 2000, with dramatic increases among the Pentecostal Evangélicos.[85]

Conclusion

European exploration and the work of Western Christian missionaries contributed to the spread of the gospel in the non-Western world during the early-modern and modern period. Western missionaries used the conveniences of colonialism to spread the gospel, but their primary mission was gospel proclamation. Men, but mostly women, ordained clergy, laypersons, doctors, nurses, linguists, educators, those with some education and others from prestigious universities boarded ships bound for the non-Western world. However, a "surprising work of God" swept parts of Asia, Africa, and Latin America during the twentieth century contributing to significant growth. While precise estimates are difficult, it is not an exaggeration to say that most of the growth of the church in the Global South that has occurred during the twentieth century is the result of non-Western revival and indigenous Christian witness. Western Missionaries may have planted the seed, but Africans, Asians, and Latin Americans have watered it. And God gave the increase.

Next we turn our attention to "the unfinished task" of world evangelism.

85. Johnson and Zurlo, "Brazil," in *World Christian Encyclopedia* (2020), 135.

5

The Unfinished Task

Why the Mission to Save the World Remains Unfinished

"The task of the church is an unfinished task, and always will be."

—Stephen Neill, *The Unfinished Task* (1957)

The British academic Stephen Neill (1900–1984) is probably best known for his classic 1964 work *A History of Christian Missions*. His book became the standard introductory text on Christian missions and is still widely used by laypersons and students alike. Neill was a respected historian with a Cambridge pedigree who published more than fifty works on missions and theology. Before embarking on his prodigious writing career he served in South India for more than twenty years as a missionary, educationalist, and bishop.[1] Neill's lesser-known work, *The Unfinished Task* (1957), was no less influential. Similar to the experiences of Andrew Walls in West Africa and David Barrett in East Africa, Stephen Neill had a front row seat to the expansive growth of the church in the Global South while serving in India during the 1940s

1. Daughrity, *Bishop Stephen Neill* (2008).

and 1950s. In his 1957 work on the church's "unfinished task," he noted that "for the first time in history, the Diaspora [the church spread around the world] has become very nearly world-wide."[2] In the late 1950s, Neill was already talking about worldwide Christianity. At the same time he emphasized that there was much work to do. As he put it in his opening salvo, "The task of the Church is the unfinished task."[3]

The Unfinished Task was in such demand that it underwent several reprints in the 1960 and 1970s. Neill's sagacious insights provided a helpful framework for thinking about the question of missions in the context of World Christianity. He recognized that Christianity had become a worldwide movement in an unprecedented way, but he also wanted to stress that the church's task remained unfinished. He pointed to the need for the church to continue to push forward into "frontier situations" utilizing "flexible ministries" in order to reach those who had never heard the gospel.[4] He was urging the church not to lose sight of its mission to the unreached. He drew attention to "the enormous growth in the population of the world" and beckoned the church to remain focused on the work of evangelism and discipleship.[5] Neill also warned about the "unknown and menacing world of secularism," expressing his immense gratitude to the work of the famed evangelist Billy Graham, while also stating that the "achievement is limited" among the "intellectual elite" and the growing "secularized civilization" of the West.[6] He also discussed the state of the "younger churches" (these are the mission-established churches in the non-Western world), while fully cognizant of the risk that his words might seem patronizing. He believed that the older churches in the West had a responsibility (and opportunity) to be engaged in leadership development and biblical discipleship in the non-Western church. Neill was in many ways ahead of his time in

2. Neill, *The Unfinished Task*, 32.
3. Neill, *The Unfinished Task*, 7.
4. Neill, *The Unfinished Task*, 53.
5. Neill, *The Unfinished Task*, 53.
6. Neill, *The Unfinished Task*, 103, 109.

the late 1950s and his central thesis remains relevant for the early twenty-first century: although the church is growing rapidly in the non-Western world, it must remain focused on the "unfinished task."

UNREACHED PEOPLE

In 1957, Neill called on the church to be engaged in "frontier situations" or what we today call unreached people groups (UPGs). During much of the modern period, the church has focused on efforts to take the gospel to "foreign countries" or non-Western nations. William Cary's 1792 work, *An Enquiry into the Obligations of Christians to Use Means for the Conversion of Heathens*, provided an explanation of the "religious state of the different nations of the world" urging the church to consider "further undertakings" for the purpose of converting the "heathens."[7] Following in Carey's wake, nineteenth-century missionaries would focus on establishing a gospel presence in every country of the world. In 1900, John Mott penned his highly influential work *The Evangelization of the World in This Generation* in which he called upon all people to "have a vision of the unevangelized world and an intense longing for the salvation" of those who have never heard the gospel. The expression "heathen" nations, with its ethnocentric overtones, was gradually replaced with "unoccupied fields" in the early twentieth century, though the strategy remained the same: the work of missions was largely focused on gaining entrée into new *nations* or "occupying" what were often called the "foreign fields" (non-Western lands) of the world. The idea of "occupying" a nation or foreign field was advanced in a 1911 work titled *Unoccupied Fields of Africa and Asia*, written by the American missionary-scholar Samuel M. Zwemer (1862–1952). The language of "occupation," with its overt reference to military strategy, created alarm in many parts of the non-Western world, gradually falling into disuse.[8] From

7. Carey, *An Enquiry* (1792).

8. A special thanks to Brian Stanley for bringing this important development to my attention.

the 1790s to the 1970s the Western church has largely focused on establishing a viable witness in every non-Christian *nation* of the world, and where possible "occupying" those nations for Christian witness. This way of thinking is now passé in the modern era of World Christianity.

A new way of thinking about the "mission field" emerged in the second half of the twentieth century. Donald McGavran (1897–1990), who studied at Yale Divinity School and Columbia University, first introduced the expression "people movement" in his 1955 work *The Bridges of God*. McGavran based his book on field research he had conducted during his work as a missionary during the Dornakal Revival in India in the 1920s and 1930s. Arguing from the Acts narrative, especially Paul's efforts to "build bridges" to Jews as well as gentiles, he coined the expression "homogenous unit principle." This, as he explained, is the theory that people are more likely to convert to Christianity when they do so as a "homogenous unit" with other people of similar demographics. (His research was later applied to the Church Growth Movement in the United States.) The concept of the church's mission to "occupy nations" was gradually replaced with its responsibility to evangelize people or people groups.

The mission strategist Ralph D. Winter (1924–2009), building on McGavran's research, was on a mission to change the way the Western church had been thinking about global evangelism. The Princeton-educated scholar, who also held a doctorate in linguistics and statistics from Cornell, sounded like an Old Testament prophet as he reproved the church for what he called "people blindness." The church, he argued, was not called to "occupy nations" but to take the gospel to all "people" or "people groups" in the world. Winter lectured the church to stop thinking about the world in terms of national boundaries and to begin thinking about people groups or cultures. If the church was only thinking about going to another nation, it was blind to the realization that within every nation there are many different people groups or cultures.

An example from Donald McGavran's place of missionary service may prove helpful. India's boundaries are a mixture of geological features (oceans, mountains, rivers) and the legacy of British colonial rule, the latter effected during the Partition of India in 1947. While India is one nation, its people speak twenty-two different languages in more than 720 different dialects! There is a vibrant Christian witness in the *nation* of India, while most of the *people* (cultures) of India remain completely cut off from the gospel. This was Winter's main argument: while every *country* in the world may have a gospel witness in some form, this does not mean that all *people/cultures* have access to the gospel. The otherwise composed scholar sounded almost frustrated by the ignorance of the Western church and the negative implications for missions. As he put it:

> Why is this fact not more widely known? I'm afraid that all our exultation about the fact that every country in the world has been penetrated has allowed many to suppose that every *culture* has been penetrated. This misunderstanding is a malady so widespread that it deserves a special name. Let us call it "people blindness," that is blindness to the existence of separate people within countries—a blindness, I might add, that seems more prevalent in the U.S. and among U.S. missionaries than anywhere else.[9]

Winter pointed out that the English word *nation* should not be confused with the Greek word for nation (*ethnē*), the latter referring not to a modern-day country, but to *an ethnic group*. Jesus did not command the church to occupy every country, but to proclaim the good news to every ethnic group (nation) so that people from "every nation, tribe, people, and language" would know and love and worship their Creator![10] The goal of missions is the worship of God through the intended and eternal diversity of all people and cultures in the kingdom of God.[11]

9. Winter, "The New Macedonia: A Revolutionary New Era in Mission Begins," 302.

10. Matt 28:18–20; Acts 1:8–10.

11. Piper, *Let the Nations Be Glad*, 177–224.

In an effort to provide better guidance for the church, mission thinkers who were influenced by Winter's insights created slogans, drew up maps, and provided popular definitions for unreached people groups (UPGS). A 1980 missions conference convened in Edinburgh adopted the slogan, "A church for every people by the year 2000." The "A.D. 2000 Movement" was born and greater attention was drawn toward church planting among the unreached.[12] In 1990, "The 10/40 Window" became the movement's map, being defined as those countries lying between 10 degrees and 40 degrees latitude, from West Africa to Japan. The map represented the largest concentration of unreached people groups in the world.[13] The most popular definition of an unreached people group in the 1990s was any ethnic group of people living in a country with an Evangelical presence of less than 1 percent.[14] (A definition that is naturally biased toward Evangelical expressions of Christianity.) In recent years, mission leaders have opted for expressions like "unengaged people groups" or "frontier people groups" to refer to those on the very fringes of unreached people groups—those who do not even know a Christian—Catholic, Orthodox, Protestant, or Evangelical! Others prefer the expression "unreached places" in order to fold into the definition the explosive growth of megacities outside of the 10/40 window with high concentrations of people that are largely unreached by the gospel.[15] The research that is being churned out by mission thinkers now estimates that of the world's 7.5 billion people, more than 3.1 billion remain culturally cut off from the gospel.[16] The Joshua Project, a mission think-tank that focuses on "bringing definition to the unfinished task," reports that of the more than 17,000 people groups in the world, more

12. Starling, *Seeds of Promise: World Consultation on Frontier Missions*, 9.

13. Coote, "'AD 2000' and the '10/40 Window': A Preliminary Assessment," 160–66.

14. Coote, "'AD 2000' and the '10/40 Window': A Preliminary Assessment," 162.

15. Shellnutt, "Why Mission Experts are Redefining 'Unreached People Groups,'" *Christianity Today* (April 22, 2019).

16. Lewis, "Clarifying the Remaining Frontier Mission Task," 158.

than 7,000 remain unreached.[17] While Christianity has expanded all over the world during the twentieth century, nearly half of the world's people have never heard a clear presentation of the gospel. The church's task remains unfinished.

UNCHANGED PERCENTAGES

When Neill penned his work in 1957 there were less than 3 billion people in the world. Today, the world's population is around 7.5 billion people. Between 1900 and 2000 Christianity grew exponentially, spreading to nearly every nation in the world. However, though the total number of Christians in the world increased dramatically in the twentieth century, the overall percentage of Christians remained unchanged. Christianity has demonstrated a pattern of numerical growth over the past two millennia, though its share in the global population has ebbed and flowed with the tides of time. The gospel expanded rapidly in the first and second centuries, so that by the year 200 AD there were 4.7 million Christians in the world, comprising 2.4 per cent of the earth's population. By the year 600 AD, just a few decades before the rise of Islam, more than 20 percent of the world's population identified in some way with the Christian faith. Christianity was geographically and ethnically diverse, spread out across North Africa, the Middle East, South Asia (India and Sri Lanka), Turkey, and Europe. One must imagine the statistical center of Christianity being somewhere in the Eastern Mediterranean, near Crete or Syria, with some 40 million Christians on a scatter plot spread out from India to the Iberian Peninsula (East to West), and from Constantinople (Istanbul) to Khartoum, North Sudan (North to South). The rise and spread of Islam across the Middle East, North Africa, and into the Iberian Peninsula between the 630s and 1450s, as well as the Black Death in the high Middle Ages, reduced the number of Christians to 16 per cent of the global population. Christianity regained its strength in the sixteenth century during the Protestant

17. The Joshua Project: https://joshuaproject.net.

and Catholic reformations, reaching the 100 million mark by the year 1600, and climbing again to more than 20 percent of the world's population by 1650.[18] Between 1800 and 1900, during the first century of the modern missionary era, the percentage of the world's Christians increased from 22 percent to 34 percent, reaching the highest overall percentage in Christian history. The number of Christians increased exponentially during the twentieth century, from 558 million to more than 2 billion, but the percentage of people who self-identify as followers of Christ remained about the same in 2000, hovering right around one-third of the world's population.[19] The gospel message is spreading more widely, but Christianity has barley kept pace with rapid populations growths in the modern world.

The unchanged percentage in the number of Christians in the world during the twentieth century may be due to the rise of secularism in Western Europe, the challenges of converting people from other religions to the faith, and the continued assignment of missionaries to regions of the world that have already been missionized.[20] On a theological note, the church should not view human population growth as a curse, but as a blessing, even if there are associated difficulties.[21] In the very beginning, God "blessed" Adam and Eve "and said to them: 'Be fruitful and increase in number; fill the earth and rule over it.'"[22] The Creator envisioned a full earth from the very beginning, and his vision for the new world is recorded for us as "a great multitude that no one could number, from every nation, tribe, people, and language."[23] Population growth represents God's blessing upon the human race and an

18. Barrett and Johnson, *World Christian Trends*, 97.

19. Johnson and Zurlo, *World Christian Encyclopedia* (2020), 4.

20. Steffan, "The Surprising Countries Most Missionaries Are Sent From and Go To," *Christianity Today* (July 25, 2013).

21. Becker, "A Christian Response to Overpopulation," *Christianity Today* (May 25, 2011). While this article provides a helpful corrective, it still dwells on the negative aspects of population growth.

22. Gen 1:28.

23. Rev 7:9.

opportunity for the church to gather more worshippers from all over the world. The church is growing, but so is the global population. The church's task remains unfinished.

UNTRAINED LEADERS

Neill laid out the need for working with the non-Western church to equip leaders for the unfinished task. In 2010, more than fifty years after his work, the Center for the Study of Global Christianity launched a worldwide survey in collaboration with 7,000 theological institutions around the world.[24] The purpose was to look quantitatively at how well the church was doing in the work of equipping leaders, especially in the non-Western world. One of the most alarming discoveries of the study was that 95 percent of the world's ministers had received no theological education, even though the mission community had been trying to address this need.[25] Some level of access to theological education is essential to the health and growth of the global church. What the church and its leaders think about God, Jesus, the Holy Spirit, the human condition, race, sexuality, sin, suffering, poverty, salvation, hope, the church, the future, and an array of other interrelated topics, has present and even eternal consequences for people. This is one of the reasons James wrote: "Not many of you should become teachers . . . because those who teach will be judged with greater strictness."[26] As the context makes clear, teachers will be judged more strictly because their words have the power to bless a life—or even destroy a life. Every Christian leader should "study to show himself approved unto God" in order to "save his own life" and the "lives of his hearers."[27] Everyone who provides leadership for the church should receive some kind of preparation for service—even

24. "Global Survey on Theological Education," World Council of Churches (2013).

25. "What Percentage of Pastor's Worldwide Have Theological Training?" Center for the Study of Global Christianity.

26. Jas 3:1

27. 2 Tim 2:15; 1 Tim 2:14–16.

if it is rudimentary in nature. The church's failure to adequately address the need for ministerial formation (equipping those who provide spiritual leadership) has already had devastating consequences. Some non-Western nations have even starting clamping down on pastors without theological training because of the negative effects that ill-equipped ministers are having on society.[28] Even secular governments in the non-Western world are realizing that when pastors do not have a theological education, their leadership can be damaging to those who follow them.

Theological education for non-Western men and women is one of the majority church's greatest needs, yet most of the world's Christian leaders are geographically and economically cut off from the opportunity to study theology and ministry leadership. During the twentieth century, as Christianity was entering an era of unprecedented expansion, the Western church made efforts to address this problem. Missionaries, denominations, and Western mission societies worked to establish non-Western theological seminaries. These efforts have had some impact, but there are simply not enough institutions to address the needs of the rapidly expanding church. Further, most theological schools in the developing world are underfunded, understaffed, and unstable.[29] In the late 1950s, during decolonization in Africa and Asia, John D. Rockefeller helped established the Theological Education Fund (TEF) with an initial grant of 2 million dollars to provide scholarships for ministry leaders. Through the generous funding of the TEF over a period of two decades there emerged a new generation of non-Western theological educators, many of whom studied overseas. However, in the absence of stable non-Western

28. Fihlani, "Why Some African Governments Are Clamping Down on Churches," *BBC News*, February 7, 2016; "Rwanda Church Closures: Pastors Arrested for Defying Order," *BBC News*, March 6, 2018.

29. Carpenter, "'To Be Agents of Life-Giving Transformation:' Christian Higher Education in Africa," Day Lecture, Annual Meeting of the Yale-Edinburgh Group, Yale Divinity School, June 28, 2019 (unpublished paper). I'm grateful to Joel Carpenter for sending me a copy of his paper.

theological schools there are few places for trained theologians to carry out their work.[30]

Efforts to bring pastors and ministry leaders to the West for training has had mixed results, with some leaders returning to serve their national churches with distinction, but many remaining in the West after finishing their education, thus creating a brain-drain effect for parts of the non-Western church.[31] Langham Partnership, a ministry founded in 1969 by the visionary leadership of John Stott (1921–2001), has had better results, requiring students to sign a declaration of intent to return to the non-Western church for service after completing their doctorates. However, Langham's work primarily exists to equip scholars, many of whom matriculate at the universities of Edinburgh, Cambridge, and Oxford, or institutions like Fuller Theological Seminary and Trinity Evangelical Divinity School.[32] These well-trained academics have a vitally important role to play in serving the global church, but only a handful of ministry leaders in the developing world will ever be able to study at a Western academic institution of higher learning, and the majority of the world's pastors will even find it difficult to study at a non-Western seminary. In the late 1960s, educators began to experiment with a scheme that became known as TEE (Theological Education by Extension), a form of distance learning whereby experienced lecturers travelled to remote regions of the world to teach short courses for pastors and ministry leaders. The concept of TEE has proven to be one of the most effective ways to make theological education accessible to non-Western leaders, and has significant promise for the future of training global leaders.[33] While the mission community is aware that theological education is one of the church's greatest needs, it is still grappling with how

30. Esterline, "From Western Church to World Christianity: Developments in Theological Education in the Ecumenical Movement," 13–22.

31. "Globalization and the Gospel: Rethinking Mission in the Contemporary World," Lausanne Occasional Paper 30, Pattaya, Thailand (2004).

32. Shaw, "John Stott and the Langham Scholarship Programme," 308–26.

33. Mubulaki, "Diversified Theological Education: Genesis, Development, and Ecumenical Potential of Theological Education by Extension," 251–62.

to meet this need. *Operation World*, arguably the most widely used popular resource for laypersons who are passionate about global missions, calls "Leadership—the key" to the Great Commission, observing that "those who accurately and effectively expound the Scriptures are few, especially in areas where the churches are growing rapidly."[34] Phrases like "mature Christian leaders are in short supply,"[35] "leadership training is the vital need,"[36] "the denominations have a leadership crisis,"[37] "the training of Christians workers is fundamental for the health and growth of the Church,"[38] and "theological training is the greatest source of weakness for the Church"[39] are repeated throughout *Operation World*. The church's task remains unfinished.

Where do we go from here?

Christianity is now firmly rooted in the soils of every continent of the world and is growing rapidly in the non-Western world. Still, the work of the church remains unfinished. There are more than 7,000 unreached people groups in the world today, which represents over 3 billion people who have never heard the name of Jesus Christ. Global population surged in the twentieth century, and currently numbers more than 7.5 billion people. While the number of Christians in the world is increasing exponentially, so is the sheer number of unbelievers. Christianity is barely growing at the rate of the global population. In the Global South, where Christianity is growing most rapidly, the younger churches are struggling to keep up with the demand for mature leaders. The negative effects of Christian leaders who do not have adequate theological training is a cause for alarm. Even in this new era of

34. Johnstone and Mandryk, *Operation World* (2001), 11.
35. Johnstone and Mandryk, *Operation World* (2001), 276.
36. Johnstone and Mandryk, *Operation World* (2001), 393.
37. Johnstone and Mandryk, *Operation World* (2001), 306.
38. Johnstone and Mandryk, *Operation World* (2001), 314.
39. Johnstone and Mandryk, *Operation World* (2001), 417.

world Christianity, the church's task remains unfinished. However, the Western church cannot carry out this work alone. In the same work, Neill also reminded the church that "the unfinished task" is the responsibility of the *whole* church. Toward the conclusion of his work, he argued that the Western church and the younger churches needed to work on the "unfinished task" with a "sense of togetherness that excludes the feeling of inferiority on the part of some, and the resentment which the sense of inferiority always kindles."[40] It is *our* unfinished task and the need for a "sense of togetherness" in the work of global missions has never been greater. It is to this subject of working together that we turn in our final two chapters.

40. Neill, *The Unfinished Task*, 160.

6

The White Man's Burden

Why the West Cannot Save the Rest and Should Not Try

Take up the White Man's burden—
Send forth the best ye breed—
Go bind your sons to exile
To serve the captive's need;
To wait in heavy harness,
On fluttered folk and wild—
Your new-caught, sullen peoples,
Half-devil and half-child.

—Rudyard Kipling (1899)

I WAS BORN IN June 1967 in south Texas. It was dubbed the Summer of Love as thousands of young people made their way to San Francisco calling for America to "make love, not war."[1] But the same summer has also been known by another name: "the long,

1. Heale, *The Sixties in America*, 97, 141; McWilliams, *The 1960s Cultural Revolution*, 70–72, 87.

hot summer of 1967." Heated racial tensions erupted in violent protests in more than 150 American cities during the summer of 1967, fuelled largely by low wages and poor housing conditions in urban areas.[2] The Johnson administration sent U.S. military personnel to the streets of America to restore peace, even while it was deploying more troops to South Vietnam. *The New York Times* reported in July 1967 that in the city of Detroit "Negro snipers waged a daylight guerrilla operation yesterday, but National Guard tanks and armored personnel carriers brought the situation under control last night."[3] There were calls for love during the summer of 1967, but for many Americans it was all-out war that summer; not only in the dense forests of Vietnam, but also in the crowded streets of America's major cities.

I still recall hearing racist comments as a young boy, many from friends and relatives who were regular church attenders. I faithfully went to Sunday school, Vacation Bible School, and Church Camp—and remember joyfully singing (and believing) that Jesus loved the little children of the world, "red and yellow black and white they are precious in his sight." We would not use the same language today, but it was good theology, even if it failed to translate into the everyday attitudes, idioms, and actions of the followers of Christ. Growing up in a very conservative Protestant tradition, I heard many sermons about all the bad things hippies were doing to our nation, but I am unable to recount a single sermon (or even discussion) about the evils of racism.

A fallacy that has been widely accepted by many Christians is that culture is something that is *out there*, a form or substance that the faithful either avoid or embrace, or in some cases try to work to transform. This framework for thinking about the relationship between followers of Christ and the wider culture was expounded in the highly influential work *Christ and Culture*, written by the American theologian Richard Niebuhr and first published in 1951. Niebuhr's work deserves praise for providing the church with a

2. Gonsalves, "The 'Long, Hot Summer of 1967,'" *The Week*, August 2, 1997.

3. Roberts, "Detroit Riots Reported Curbed after Tanks Fight Day Snipers; Death Toll at 36," *New York Times*, July 27, 1967.

framework for thinking about culture and his work was ahead of its time. But as the American historian George Marsden pointed out, some fifty years later, the problem with this way of framing culture is that Christians themselves are "culturally conditioned."[4] We *are* able to think about the culture around us, but at best we are all observer-participants. Most of us are probably less like Auguste Rodin's iconic bronze statute *The Thinker*—reflecting on the world around us and unchanged by our surroundings—and more like the proverbial frog in the kettle. The temper of our cultural surrounds has a subtle way of conditioning us. The bigoted Nathan Price may not be a fair representative of the typical missionary, but Western missionaries during the modern period were culturally conditioned to some degree by contemporary assumptions regarding nation and race. However, in an expected turn of events, many of the same missionaries who went out to change the world, also returned home changed by their experiences abroad.

THE WHITE MAN'S BURDEN

Rudyard Kipling (1865–1936) was an English writer born in British India. He travelled extensively throughout the British Empire, though he lived most of his life in the cities of London and Bombay.[5] In 1899, Kipling's poem "The White Man's Burden" was published in American newspapers as a celebration of the superiority of Western culture and the goodness of imperialism.[6] It was the year after America's conflict with Spain during the Cuban

4. Marsden, "Christianity and Cultures: Transforming Niebuhr's Categories," 6. Marsden was providing a critique of *Christ and Culture* on the fiftieth anniversary of Niebuhr's lectures which had been given at Austin Theological Seminary in January 1949.

5. "Rudyard Kipling (1865–1936)," *The Oxford Companion to English Literature*, 808.

6. The poem appeared in several hundred newspapers across the United States early in 1899. A few examples include: *Daily Republican*, January 30, 1899, *The Sun*, February 1, 1899, *The Saint Paul Globe*, February 1, 1899, *The Kansas City Journal*, February 2, 1899, *The Salt Lake Herald*, February 5, 1899 and *The San Francisco Call*, February 5, 1899.

War of Independence, which led to the Philippine-American War (1899–1902). Kipling's poem was a serenade, an anthem in praise of colonialism, urging the United States to do its duty by seizing control of Spanish territories. The British poet sang of the white man's duty to bring salvation to those non-Western inhabitants, likening them to wild beasts—"fluttered folk and wild." They were, as he put it, "half-devil and half-child." It was, in his view, virtuous for Western nations to send "the best" of their "breed" to conquer foreign lands in order to serve the "captive's need." War and foreign rule were necessary to bring peace so that the white man could "fill full the mouth of famine" and "bid the sickness cease." Kipling's worldview was in vogue at the turn of the twentieth century, and in 1907 he was awarded the Nobel Prize for his literary work.[7] Racial superiority and national chauvinism (extreme forms of nationalism) were acceptable sentiments in Great Britain and the United States in Kipling's day. While missionaries were primarily focused on evangelistic work (see chapter 3), the Western missionary movement was carried out within a cultural milieu that tacitly accepted the notion that the "white man" was providentially chosen by God to save the "wild beasts" of the world. Western emissaries were on a mission to convert rather than colonize, but they were working within a historical context that accepted the superiority of Western culture.

ALL HAVE SINNED

In the late nineteenth century, theologians and mission enthusiasts adhered to the notion that America and Great Britain were providentially chosen by God to save the world.[8] These views were especially strong in the United States, where America was often described as "exceptional" (thus the expression "American exceptionalism"), a "City on a Hill" that was providentially chosen by

7. "Rudyard Kipling (1865–1936)," *The Oxford Companion to English Literature*, 808.

8. Littlefield, *Chosen Nations*, (2013).

God to be a light to the nations.[9] As Austin Phelps put it in the foreword to Josiah Strong's 1891 theological work *Our Country*: "As goes America, so goes the world. The United States [is] first and foremost the chosen seat of enterprise for the world's conversion."[10] Religious leaders in Great Britain held similar views. As the Welsh Methodist Hugh Price Hughes (1847–1902) put it in 1902, "the English language, the English political tendency, and above all the English conception of Christianity will rule the world."[11]

The notion that the Western world had been "chosen by God" to save the rest of the world is not inherently racist (even if it is theologically suspect), though it is easy to see how such a worldview might lead to attitudes of racial superiority and national chauvinism. This was in fact a problem in biblical Israel, where the concept of "being chosen" was confused with national and ethnic superiority expressed in racist views toward those who were not of pure Jewish decent. In contrast, the doctrine of election (in both testaments) was/is intended to produce humility and love for people of all races—Jew and gentile. It may be that many Western Christians during the twentieth century have committed the same sins of their forefathers, perhaps at times unwittingly embracing the notion of national (Western) superiority. In any event, it is fair to say that political and religious leaders in the United States and Great Britain believed that they were called of God to "save the world" and this deeply held cultural conviction often expressed itself in racial superiority and national chauvinism.[12] While most missionaries were not on a mission to conquer the world for their own nation (as we have already demonstrated), they often subscribed to the notion that it was their duty to take up "the white man's burden" by taking the gospel out to the heathen of the world—the "sullen" and "wild," the "half-deviled, half-child."

9. McKenzie, "The Most Famous Metaphor of American Exceptionalism Is a Warning, Not a Boast," *Christianity Today*, November 21, 2018.

10. Strong, *Our Country*, 14.

11. Hugh Price Hughes, *Methodist Times* 18 (January 2, 1902) 8.

12. Edwards, "Forging an Ideology for American Missions: Josiah Strong and Manifest Destiny," 163–91.

WORLD CHRISTIANITY AND RACISM

In 1903 W. E. B. Du Bois (1868–1963) penned his classic work *The Souls of Black Folk.* His forward began with the prescient words: "the problem of the Twentieth Century is the problem of the color line."[13] Racism, as Du Bois predicted, remained a problem throughout the twentieth century, even though some Western missionaries, missionary children (called MKs), and political activists began to denounce its evils.[14] During the 1930s, German Protestant theology and the German Evangelical Church became unlikely bedfellows with Third Reich ideology and Hitler's racist policies.[15] Pope Pius XII (r. 1939–58), also known as "Hitler's pope," in his effort to remain neutral, was unwilling to use the papal pulpit to condemn the inhumane policies of the Third Reich.[16] By contrast, Dietrich Bonhoeffer's opposition to Hitler's hatred was extraordinary, and he was martyred for his activism. Following the Second World War, racism was an acceptable sin even among many Evangelical Christians. Evangelist Billy Graham (1918–2018) did not "tear down the ropes" of his largely segregated audiences in the South until 1953. Graham's willingness to defy the socially accepted practice of preaching to segregated audiences created a stir among white clergymen throughout the 1950s.[17] The Evangelical theologian John Piper (b. 1946), speaking of his years growing up in the American south in the 1950s, confessed, "I was, in those years, manifestly racist."[18] The mission I examined during my doctoral studies, which became the largest Protestant mission agency on the African continent in the twentieth century, was in turmoil over how to handle the issue of racial integration in

13. Du Bois, *Du Bois' Writings*, 359.

14. For a succinct and helpful introduction to the history of racism, see Rattansi, *Racism: A Very Short Introduction* (2020)

15. Bergen, *Twisted Cross: The German Christian Movement in the Third Reich* (1996).

16. Stanley, *A World History of Christianity in the Twentieth Century*, 156–57.

17. Wacker, *America's Pastor*, 121–31.

18. Piper, *Bloodlines*, 33.

the 1950s. Executives balked at the suggestion by some of its missionaries that it should accept "colored Evangelicals" as full-fledge members of the mission community. Officials in the home office wondered aloud (mostly in closed-door meetings) about how they would address the question of equal compensation as well as the problem that would be posed when the children of black American missionaries wanted to attend school with the children of their white colleagues. Mission authorities suggested that perhaps they could create separate mission stations that "were staffed entirely by negroes" in Africa.[19] The "problem of the color bar" was a problem even among Christians and Christian mission societies during the first half of the twentieth century.

THE "GLOBAL CIVIL RIGHTS MOVEMENT"

After the horrors of the Second World War global attitudes on race began to change as secular and religious leaders called for both civil rights and an end to white rule. While historians usually recount the civil rights movement in the United States with little reference to events in the wider world, religious and secular leaders of the period understood American civil rights as part of part of a larger campaign against global racism.[20] Attitudes of ethnic superiority were pervasive throughout the Western world, and white, colonial rule was viewed as an expression of the racist worldview. In 1942, a chorus of Protestant leaders began calling for the equality "of other races in our own and other lands."[21] In 1947, two years after the war ended, the Lutheran theologian Otto Frederick Nolde produced a series of essays arguing for global racial equality, calling for the church to lead the way:

19. Barnett, "Acceptance of Negro Missionaries from U.S.A. to Kenyan Field," Africa Inland Mission, Kenyan Field Report, April 16–21, 1951; George Van Dusen to R. T. Davis, Rethy, Congo, June 1, 1951.

20. An exception to this general neglect of the global context of American racism is Kendi, *Stamped from the Beginning*, 308–22, 349–65.

21. Hollinger, *After Cloven Tongues of Fire*, 56–81.

> The Christian gospel relates to all men, regardless of race, language or color. . . . [T]here is no Christian basis to support a fancied intrinsic superiority of any one race. The rights of all peoples of all lands should be recognized and safeguarded. International cooperation is needed to create conditions under which these freedoms may become a reality.[22]

The call for racial equality was part of a worldwide movement that demanded freedom for "all peoples of all lands." In 1948, the global community adopted the Universal Declaration of Human Rights (UDHR), a watershed event in the worldwide battle against racism. American Protestant missionaries were highly influential in the language of the UDHR and became vocal proponents for religious freedom as well as global human rights.[23] Attitudes were shifting in the Western world and missionaries were helping lead the way. Du Bois, who is perhaps best known as an American civil rights activist, is more properly understood as a prophetic voice calling for an end to global racism and white oppression. Though he was an atheist, Dubois worked alongside Western missionaries in the adoption of the UDHR in 1948 and expressed his belief that Western missionaries had an important role to play in putting an end to global racism. Du Bois was also an influential Pan-Africanist, a twentieth-century movement of international activists who were working to "unite and uplift" all people of African descent and free African colonies from Western rule. Early Pan-Africanist leaders who worked with Du Bois included Kwame Nkrumah (1909–72), an African revolutionary who became Ghana's first Prime Minister in 1957, and Jomo Kenyatta (1897–1978), an anti-colonial activist who served as Kenya's first president.[24] Du Bois travelled widely in North America, Europe, Africa, and Asia, and understood the battle for civil rights in the United States as part of a worldwide struggle for human freedom.

22. Nolde, *Toward World-Wide Christianity*, 142.

23. Moyn, *Christian Human Rights* (2015).

24. Cambell, "Pan-Africanism," in *A Concise Oxford Dictionary of Politics and International Relations* (2018).

In point of fact, global developments on racism directly influenced American civil rights policies. American politicians in both the Kennedy and Johnson administration felt international pressure to clean up the nation's image in order to win the allegiance of African and Asian nations.[25] Communism was attractive to many nations in Africa and Asia that had been under the yoke of Western rule because of its strong solidarity with the plight of the poor. Interestingly, in the 1940s Du Bois had hoped that African Americans would lead the way for the freedom movements on the African continent, but by 1961 his experiences abroad convinced him that "Africans may have to show American Negroes the way to freedom."[26] Racism was a global problem and the call for civil rights was a worldwide movement.

Something I became more aware of as I was toiling away in dusty archives was that changing attitudes on global human rights and white rule became a crisis for some missionaries and mission societies even as they tried to remain focused on their primary work of gospel proclamation. As an example, the mission I became most familiar with was forced to reposition itself due to the rise of nationalism and anti-white sentiment in the 1950s during the Mau Mau Conflict (ca. 1952–56). The changes sweeping the African continent created political pressure to "Africanize" all spheres of society (including the church). In the decade that followed Kenyan independence from Great Britain (the process began in about 1958 and independence was announced in 1963), the all-white mission initially resisted pressure from African church leaders for a peaceful hand over of its property and power. In spite of assurances otherwise, missionaries feared they would then be pressured to leave the country (thus ending their work). The mission finally relinquished its authority in the 1970s after African church leaders threatened a hostile take over, though it was not until 1980 that a complete hand-over over had taken place due to the demand of the African church's stalwart bishop, who grew weary of what he

25. Skrentny, "The Effect of the Cold War on African-American Civil Rights," 256.

26. Du Bois, "American Negroes and Africa's Rise to Freedom," 216.

called the "mission station mentality." (He was referring to the failure of missionaries to fully "integrate" with the African church.) Foreign control by whites—whether in the nation, the church, or mission societies—was out of step with the times. Even mission organizations that were not fully on board with the changing times brought by decolonization were forced to adjust.

It is important for Western Christians who are engaged in world missions to understand that white supremacy in all its forms has been rejected by the non-Western world. During the second half of the twentieth century missionaries who were serving in the non-Western world were the ones most keenly aware of this global mood. Throughout the African continent, during the second half of the twentieth century, colonies rebelled against their Western masters buoyed by the fight for human freedom and the end of global racism. As former colonies became independent, Western missionaries from various denominations, Catholic and Protestant, were forced to relinquish ecclesiastical authority. The transitions "from mission to church" (referred to as "devolution") in various denominations were often tense and uneven. Progressive voices within mission circles called for devolution as soon as possible. Max Warren (1904–77), who served as the vicar of Holy Trinity, Cambridge from 1936 to 1942, and the general secretary of the Church Missionary Society from 1942 to 1963, was especially persuasive in convincing the global mission community to adjust to the changes sweeping the world during decolonization.[27] In most cases, missionaries and mission societies responded with alacrity, preparing local leaders for positions of authority as quickly as possible, often out of concern that they would be forced to leave the country by new government regimes that might be hostile to Western workers (as in China in 1949, and the Belgian Congo in 1960).

27. Kings, "Warren, Max," in Anderson, *Biographical Dictionary of Christian Missions*, 719; for a summary article covering Warren's influence, see Porter, "War, Colonialism and the British Experience: The Redefinition of Christian Missionary Policy, 1932–1952," 269–88.

In newly independent nations where mission societies were allowed to continue working, missionaries sometimes felt compelled to relinquish control of the church fearing that they might be perceived as anti-government or even racist.[28] Conditions in South Africa were even more complex, with church and state intertwined in private and public spheres, and racial tensions continuing well past the end of apartheid (ca. 1994) up to the present day.[29] In China and India, most Western missionaries had already been pressured to return home by 1950 due to anti-Western sentiment and mission societies had no choice but to hand over the leadership of the church to indigenous leaders. In Latin American, while nations had experienced political freedom more than a century earlier, frustrations mounted in the middle of the twentieth century over the elitism that was displayed by church hierarchy. Christian leaders, both Catholic and Protestant, expressed solidarity with the poor and oppressed through the espousal of liberation theology (ca. 1950s-1990s). This form of theology, drawing heavily on the exodus motif, argued that God is on a mission to set his people free, both spiritually *and* politically. The rhetoric of liberation theology was often anti-Western and some of the criticisms of liberation theologians were directed toward Western missionaries who were viewed as neo-colonialists. During the 1940s through the 1990s Western mission societies were pressured to adjust to the rapidly changing world around them. "White rule" in all its forms was being rejected in Africa, Asia, and Latin America.

"MISSIONARY GO HOME!"

What exactly did this mean for missions in the second half of the twentieth century? None of this will be new for those who were actually on the "mission field" (as it was called) during this period, but it is important for everyone who is passionate about missions to know this story. Following the Second World War, the

28. Hastings, *A History of African Christianity*, 108–30.

29. De Gruchy, "Religion and Racism," 385–400.

changing attitudes on racial superiority and white rule created difficult working conditions for many missionaries. In one respect, life was improving for the people those who had left kith and kin to preach the gospel in foreign lands. Planes, trains, and automobiles enabled missionaries to move about the world with greater ease. Advances in science and medicine, especially in the area of malarial prevention and treatment, significantly decreased the risk of death. Transistor radios, transatlantic air-travel, the telephone, and airmail were all bringing new conveniences to people working in the remote regions of the world. The growth of large cities in Africa, Asia, and Latin America meant that missionaries were no longer burdened by the requirement to ship all their supplies from overseas; needments could be purchased upon arrival and transported further afield. However, rebellion against the white man's rule (even in the church) created difficult working conditions for missionaries. Referring to the social and political pressure missionaries were facing during the mid-twentieth century, one mission executive wrote in 1959: "Such circumstances can be more testing and trying than were disease and danger in the pioneer days of missionary enterprise."[30] Now that the "pioneer days" of mission work were over, the more difficult task of working with the non-Western church in a changing world had begun.

Was it time for the missionary to go home now that white rule was being rejected? Opposition to white rule in the non-Western world was palpable during the second half of the twentieth century, leading sociologists to (wrongly) conclude that Christianity would be sent home along with Western missionaries. In 1964, the mission strategist James A. Scherer (1921–99) penned the book for which he became later became famous: *Missionary, Go Home!* The title of the work was intentionally provocative. Scherer was very committed to the continued work of overseas missions, but he was encouraging the Western church to re-think its role in the context of global changes. As he put it in his opening salvo, "'Missionary, Go Home!' is an attitude frequently stated or implied."[31]

30. Henman, "Power?" *Inland Africa* (April 1959), 1.

31. Scherer, *Missionary, Go Home!*, 5.

His survey of global changes during the 1950s and early 1960s led him to the conclusion that "New ways must be found to express the unchanging missionary obligation."[32] In 1966, more than 1,000 (mostly) Evangelical mission leaders gathered from all over the world in Wheaton, Illinois and declared: "We have grievously sinned." Among the sins confessed was the failure "to apply Scriptural principles" to the problem of "racism" as well as "perpetuating paternalism and provoking unnecessary tensions between national churches and missionary societies . . . ."[33] Mission-minded Christians remained committed to the work of missions, but their experiences on the field had taught them that a new day was dawning in the way Western missionaries carried out their work in the non-Western world.

In the early 1970s, calls were heard from the non-Western church for what became known as a "moratorium on missions." The prophetic voice was an African clergyman named John Gatũ (1925–2017), a committed Evangelical, a convert of the East African Revival, and the most senior leader of the Presbyterian Church in East Africa.[34] Gatũ was a mission enthusiast, but his experiences as a church leader in Africa led him to the conclusion that the continued presence of *Western* missionaries was paradoxically weakening the church throughout Africa. He believed that the long-term growth and health of the church meant that African leaders must, as he put it, "learn to stand on their own two feet" and take responsibility for missionary endeavors.[35] Gatũ's call for a moratorium on Western missions was publicized during a series of talks he gave in the United States during the early 1970s, immediately drawing the ire of American Evangelicals.[36] When Gatũ spoke at the International Congress on World Evangelism held in Lausanne in 1974, he repeated his call for a moratorium on

32. Scherer, *Missionary, Go Home!*, 5.

33. "Wheaton Declaration: Subscribed by the Delegates to the Congress on the Church's Worldwide Mission," 460.

34. Njogu, "Gatũ, John (1925–)," in *Dictionary of African Biography* (2011).

35 Gatũ, *Fan into Flame: An Autobiography*, appendix (Kindle).

36. Gatũ, *Fan into Flame: An Autobiography*, chapter 5 (Kindle).

Western missions (at a conference on world evangelism nonetheless!), much to the consternation of Billy Graham. John Stott, who enjoyed a friendship with both Graham and Gatũ, used his considerable skills of diplomacy to bring the two together, after which they departed as friends. Graham, who still could not bring himself to support Gatũ's policy, came away from Lausanne with a better understanding of Gatũ's arguments.[37] While not advocating a moratorium on missions, J. Herbert Kane (1910–88), an Evangelical missions leader and professor, emphasized the need for missionaries to make adjustments. Kane, who served with the China Inland Mission in the late 1940s, was evacuated along with his family and other missionaries in 1950 due to communist restrictions on Western missionary work. His 1973 work, *Winds of Change in the Christian Mission* published by Moody Press, was a call for the continuation of missions work while advocating the need for new strategies. His work was highly influential in the Evangelical mission community, first published in 1973, then reprinted in 1975, 1976, 1977, and 1979. In the late 1960s and throughout the 1970s, the Western church was coming to grips with its need for change. The non-Western church had embraced the gospel, but non-Western leaders were growing weary of foreign rule and unhealthy dependence on the Western church.

THE END OF OLD MODELS?

So what do these changes mean for global missions in the modern period? The 1980s and 1990s were punctuated by calls for a new way of doing missions. White-dominated approaches in Africa, Asia, and Latin America were increasingly viewed as passé. Surveying the changes sweeping the world during the post-colonial period, mission strategist Ted Ward proclaimed in 1982: "The end of old models is in sight."[38] Calls for change reverberated from missionaries and mission thinkers, though old ways of doing things

37. Reese, "John Gatũ and the Moratorium on Missionaries," 245–56.

38. Ward, "Christian Missions—Survival in What Form?" 2–3.

still persisted. Experts and expats alike wanted the church to rein in nationalism, abandon racism, and work together with the non-Western church as co-equals in the gospel. Mission strategists called for the church to abandon "the West to the rest" mentality and adopt a new way of working together that has been captured in the expression, "mission from everywhere to everyone."[39] Creighton Lacy, a missionary who had been born into a missionary family in China in 1919, observed that missionaries were trying to lead the way, but their churches back home were often lagging behind. In a 1982 work, he remarked, "Missionaries on the whole appear to be more conscious" than the "home folks" on matters related to culture and race.[40] "Home folks" did appear to be lagging behind in the late twentieth century. In 1986 one mission strategist talked about the emerging leadership in the non-Western church, but observed with evident disappointment that "global racism" remains an on-going problem.[41] In a 1999 article, another missiologist talked about the "colonial attitudes" that persist in the Western church when they act as if they can completely "by-pass the expertise and experience of local and national churches and can go anywhere they want and do anything they please."[42] A 1983 article on mission societies praises them for diversifying their leadership on the field yet opines that much of the decision making "still rests in the hands of organizations outside the country" while the local/national church is "by-passed rather than affirmed."[43] The well-known missions thinker Ralph Winter expressed his frustration with what he called the "myth of closed countries" stating that it is a "never-correct concept" and reveals our belief that a country is closed to the gospel because an *American* cannot enter! A sagacious thinker on mission strategy,

39. Escobar, *The New Global Mission: The Gospel from Everywhere to Everyone* (2003).

40. Lacy, "Toward a Post-Denominational World Church," 341.

41. Jones, "History's Lessons for Tomorrow's Mission," 53.

42. Ward, "Repositioning Mission Agencies for the Twenty-first Century," 146–52.

43. Samuel and Sugden, "Mission Agencies as Multinationals," 152–55.

Winter sounded impatient as he called for a *global* strategy to reach the unreached through "the strategic interfacing of a global mission movement."[44] Winter emphasized again that the West and the rest needed to work together to solve the problem of reaching the unreached! In 1995, reflecting on the International Congress on World Evangelism in Lausanne (1974) where Evangelicals from the global church vowed to work together in partnership for the spread of the gospel, the mission-minded Evangelical John Stott complained: "I wonder what has become of our penitence and our pledge? I can see few signs of them today."[45] Non-Western voices also chimed in. In 1989, the Ecuadorian theologian Renè Padilla called for "the set up of partnership in mission on a global scale" complaining that "paternalism still reigns supreme." He continued: "The trouble is that despite the wide recognition, in theory, of a global outlook on mission, many Western missionary societies, in practice, continue to operate as if they were living in the nineteenth century."[46] There were strong calls for an end to old models, but progress was often frustrated by old habits of the heart.

"The Waterpeople"

I learned about the growth of Christianity in the non-Western world during my sabbatical in Kenya in 2006 and I also learned a lot about the attitudes of non-Western Christians toward Western missionaries. A research project I undertook while in Kenya showed that Africans not only resented the legacy of Western control and racism (this did not surprise me), they also believed that mission societies had displayed attitudes of cultural and racial superiority. Interestingly, many Africans believed that the reluctance of Western missionaries to provide adequate ministerial

44. Winter and Motte, "Mission in the 1990s: Two Views," 100–101.

45. Stott, "Twenty Years after Lausanne: Some Personal Reflections," 53.

46. Hendricks and Padilla, "Mission in the 1990s: Two Views," 150.

preparation for local leaders was an expression of cultural and racial superiority.[47]

While I was lecturing in the church history department at the Nairobi Evangelical School of Theology that year, a pastor from Ukambani (near Machakos, Kenya) came by my cottage one evening to deliver a copy of Jo de Graft's literary masterpiece *Muntu.* The African play was performed in 1975 at the World Council of Churches gathering in Nairobi and is now considered a classic in African literature.[48] In the play, the Waterpeople arrive while the sons and daughters of Africa are fighting among themselves over how to govern their own affairs. The "First Water-man" is a Christian missionary who has come to Africa to make converts; the second is a trader who sets up a shop for buying and selling; the third is a white settler in search of land; the fourth is a colonial administrator with plans to build a railway for exporting gold.[49] The Waterpeople were brandishing muskets and even the missionary proved to be an excellent marksman. The African pastor who handed me the play explained that de Graft's work would help me understand the mindset of many Africans, especially those who were university educated.[50] Africans Christians, I was to learn, remember that the Western missionary arrived along with the settler, the trader, and the colonial administrator—often on the same ships. More discerning Christians, he informed me, understood that the missionary had different aims. However, he continued, it was important for me to understand that a new generation of African leaders had emerged who would not abide anything that resembled Western superiority. The end of white rule in non-Western nations, he wanted me to understand, also meant the end of any hint of white rule in the African church.

47. A summation of these findings were published in the *International Bulletin of Missionary Research.* See Young, "A 'New Breed of Missionaries': Assessing Attitudes toward Western Missions at the Nairobi Evangelical Graduate School of Theology," 90–95.

48. De Graft, *Muntu* (1982).

49. De Graft, *Muntu,* 34.

50. Stanley, *The Bible and the Flag* (2010).

Christians in Africa, Asia, and Latin America want (and deserve) to work with the church in the Western world as *co-equals* in the gospel for the cause of global missions. Church leaders in the non-Western world are keenly aware of the history of subjugation that they and their forefathers have endured. They do not want to be ignored, by-passed, looked-down on, or patronized by the Western church—arriving in their country to carry out their work independently as though no African, Asian, or Latin American church actually exists. They want the Western church to serve with them in common witness. They also want Western church leaders to acknowledge them, respect them, and listen to them. They want Western Christians to first understand their needs and then come and serve alongside them.[51] It is too easy to mistake the hospitality offered by the people of the non-Western world to Western visitors for willing subservience. It is critical for the Western church to understand that attitudes toward North Americans and Europeans have changed during the twentieth century and that even hospitable hosts are aware of the long history of cultural and racial superiority.

Bishop Oscar Muriu (see chapter 7) is an influential Christian leader on the African continent who has also become a personal friend. I have been the recipient of his kind hospitality on many occasions and he has been a guest in my home on more than one occasion. We have had many frank discussions over good meals. In a recent exchange, I was soliciting his counsel on a matter related to missions and he opined (again) about "all the white people from the West . . . dreaming [about missions] in the 2/3 world."[52] Our non-Western brethren want us to be engaged in mission, but they don't want to be ignored, especially when we are planning mission initiatives in their own backyard! As the Kenyan activist and photojournalist Boniface Mwangi put it in a 2015 op-ed published in the *The New York Times*: "If you want to come and help me, first ask me what I want . . . then we can

51. Young, "A New Breed of Missionaries," 90–95.

52. Muriu, e-mail message to author, December 16, 2018.

work together."[53] It is not the "The White Man's Burden" to save the world; it is the responsibility of the whole church, to take the whole gospel, to the whole world.

So where do we go from here?

53. Herrman, "An African's Message for America," *New York Times*, January 5, 2015.

7

A Century of Partnerships?

New Trends in Missions That Could Transform the World

"If you want to go fast, go alone; if you want to go far, go together."

—Swahili Proverb

THE TIDE HAS BEGUN to turn in the early twenty-first century as Western Christians are becoming more aware of the numerical growth and mission potential of the majority church. Dana Robert's cover article "Shifting Southward," published in the *International Bulletin of Missionary Research* in the year 2000, was a stake in the ground, marking a new era of thinking globally about missions, theology and the study of Christian history.[1] In 2001, Oxford published the massive second edition of the *World Christian Encyclopedia*, which provided an introductory summary, broken down by continents, on the rapid growth of Christianity in Africa, Asia, and Latin America during the past century, with exponential growth occurring since the 1970s.[2] Philip Jenkins' *The Next*

1. Robert, "Shifting Southward," *IBMR*, 50–58.
2. Barrett, *World Christian Encyclopedia*, 3–23.

Christendom: The Coming of Global Christianity was nominated by *Christianity Today* as one of the most influential works of 2003.[3] While Jenkins was drawing from readily available scholarship on the rapid growth of Christianity in the non-Western world, the claims he made were new to many of his otherwise well-informed readers. The year after its release he wrote: "When I published *The Next Christendom*, I was surprised by the public response precisely because so little of the material was terribly new, at least to anyone who had taken the trouble to observe religious trends over the previous two or three decades."[4] News about the growth and vitality of the church in the non-Western world was not new, but in the early twenty-first century the Southern shift was finally starting to make headlines.

THE COMING OF GLOBAL MISSIONS

In 2006, Oscar Muriu (mentioned in chapter 6), the man *Christianity Today* called "The African Church Planter," electrified a gathering of nearly 20,000 mission-minded university students in Urbana, Illinois.[5] Students gasped as he talked about how the church in Africa had grown from 9 million converts in the year 1900 to more than 360 million by the year 2000. They applauded as he cited passages from Jenkins' work *The Next Christendom* and rattled off statistics from the *World Christian Encyclopedia* detailing the rapid growth of Christianity in Africa, Asia, and Latin America. The room grew silent as he began talking about the erosion of traditional values in North America and Western Europe, and the decline of Christianity in parts of the Western world. He then made it clear that the changes he had just recounted meant that the Western church and the non-Western church needed to work together in new and creative ways. As he put it: "Because our

3. "2003 Christianity Today Book Awards," *Christianity Today* (June 2003), 42.

4. Jenkins, "After the Next Christendom," 20.

5. "The African Church Planter: An Interview with Oscar Muriu," *Christianity Today* (April 2007).

world is changing, our models for missions must change" observing that the church needed to reject "the older model of missions," which he described as "the West to the rest." He paused and then raised his voice: "Not so in the body!" Handsomely dressed in a traditional African kofia (hat) and dashiki (shirt), Muriu called for an end to "patronizing cultural arrogance." He encouraged students to go out and serve the world, but to "always enter another culture with the posture of learning." He called for a transformation in the way short-term mission trips were being done, exhorting Western students to come first to listen and learn. He finished his rousing speech by exclaiming: "This century must be the century of genuine partnerships and nothing else."[6]

At the beginning of the twenty first century greater effort is being made to understand some of the challenges and opportunities of partnership in mission. One significant challenge is that Western church leaders do not always understand the effect that power dynamics have on relationships. In a 2009 article, Larry Jones warned that "leaders of Western mission efforts . . . need to be conscious of the overwhelming power we bring to intercultural relationships."[7] Power dynamics are usually present, even if Western leaders are not aware of them, and this can make it difficult to navigate healthy partnerships. Those who are experimenting with partnerships are reporting that there are benefits for both Western and non-Western Christians. In a 2010 article, an American missionary to French-speaking Arabs in North Africa outlined a case study based on his "partnership" experiment that resulted in a mutually beneficial relationship between a local Arab congregation in Morocco and an Evangelical church in Grenoble, France.[8] Cross-cultural partnerships, the article argues, have the potential to strengthen both the Western and non-Western church. In 2012, Rich Starcher, a seasoned missionary and professor at Biola, offered practical advice on "how not to collaborate with a majority world church" urging Western leaders to make "relationship" the

6. Muriu, "The Global Church," Urbana 2006.

7. Jones, "The Problem of Power in Ministry Relationships," 405.

8. Kronk, "Successful Partnership: A Case Study," 180–89.

starting point.[9] Starcher notes that there must be more than an exchange of money for partnerships to be viable; friendships in the gospel need to be a high priority. In a 2014 article, two seasoned academics argued that one of the most effective ways of partnership in the global church is supporting leadership development through "partnership with majority world institutions" that are engaged in equipping and empowering nationals.[10] Their findings suggest that non-Western churches want to be empowered, not enabled. In a 2015 article, Josh Broward, drawing from his own experiences as a mission leader, observed that partnerships with the global church have "revolutionized" the ministries he has led.[11] Spiritual transformation can happen in the Western church when it works with Christians in the non-Western church.

The Roman Catholic Church, building on its catholicity (it's sense of the universal or whole church), has begun "twinning" wealthier Western parishes with non-Western congregations in the Global South. The practice of "twinning" congregations is also practiced among Protestants in Great Britain and continental Europe, though it is less known in North America. In North American Protestantism, some 86 percent of mega-churches (churches with more than 2,000 attenders) now report that they are experimenting with some kind of partnership model.[12] Theologians and missions-thinkers are beginning to think about a theology of partnership drawing on the biblical motifs of "global friendships" and the church as "the body of Christ."[13] Working together as partners, as "friends," as brothers and sisters in the same "body of Christ" has become the new direction of global missions in the twenty-first

9. Starcher, "How Not to Collaborate with a Majority World Church," 416–25.

10. Greenman and Green, "The Priority of Leadership Training in Global Mission," 44–49.

11. Broward, "Think Big, Think Small: Partnership as a Revolution in Global Missions," 180–89.

12. Priest, "U.S. Mega-churches and New Patterns of Global Mission," 97–103.

13. Robert, "Global Friendship as Incarnational Missional Practice," 145–49.

century.[14] There are encouraging signs that the Western church is gradually moving away from a Western-dominated approach to global missions.

A NEW KIND OF MISSIONARY

Mission strategist Larry Pate made a prescient observation more than thirty years ago when he stated that "the future of missions belongs to the missionaries of Latin America, Africa, Asia, and Oceania."[15] The data on world missions is complex, but there is at least one indisputable fact: the number of non-Western missionaries is rapidly increasing. In the year 1900, nearly all missionaries were sent out "from the West to the rest."[16] There are now about 425,000 cross-cultural missionaries at work around the world, and more than 200,000 of those full-time workers are being sent out from the Global South.[17] While the United States continues to increase its funding for mission initiatives, mission organizations are now spending more of their money on non-Western personnel. By the late 1990s, mission statisticians were reporting that in the United States alone, 42 percent of the workers sent out and supported by U.S. mission agencies were non-U.S. citizens. In 2005, the percentage of non-US workers supported by the Western church had risen to a staggering 68 percent.[18] While support for missions remains strong in the Western church, more funding is now going to support the work of non-Western missionaries. In the early twenty-first century, the profile of the average missionary has changed. Today it is not unusual to meet a missionary

14. Robert, *Faithful Friendships: Embracing Diversity in Christian Community* (2019).

15. Pate, *From Every People*, 5.

16. Johnson and Zurlo, "Mission," in *World Christian Encyclopedia* (2020), 32.

17. Steffan, "The Surprising Countries Most Missionaries Are Sent From and Go To," *Christianity Today*, July 25, 2013.

18. Noll, *The New Shape of World Christianity*, 116–17; Johnstone and Mandryk, *Operation World*, 46; Weber and Welliver, *Mission Handbook*, 51.

from Kenya sent by a church in Nairobi and funded by a mission organization in Colorado Springs.[19] This is one example of the experimentation that is taking place in the new era of partnerships. Missions is no longer the domain of the Western church; it is the work of the *whole* church. As an Ethiopian church leader recently said to a *Christianity Today* journalist, "Missions is not a Western responsibility; it is the church's responsibility."[20]

OUR EPHESIANS MOMENT

Andrew Walls, the doyen of World Christianity (see chapter 2), has an uncanny ability for teasing out the contemporary implications of the first-century biblical witness. In his essay titled "Our Ephesians Moment," he rehearses the first-century background of the book of Ephesians. The early church began in Jerusalem, the Scriptures were given to Israel, the church's Savior and Lord was Jewish by birth and all the church's first leaders were ethnic Jews. Yet, through Christ, those who were "gentiles by birth" are no longer "foreigners" but are "citizens" of the kingdom of God. Jews and gentiles were brought together into "one new person." The church that began in Jerusalem underwent a dramatic geographic, demographic, and cultural shift. In this "Ephesians moment" Paul was calling (and working) for unity between Jews and gentiles. Jerusalemites and Athenians, Sabbath-keepers and "rule-breakers," kosher and non-kosher, circumspect shoppers and carefree carnivores—were united in Christ. The apostle Paul exhorted the church in this "Ephesians moment" to "make every effort to be united" because there is only "one body" and "one Lord."[21] And what is at stake? Our witness. Walking worthy of our calling means that we are striving to live and serve in unity with those who are *different* from us by God's sovereign design, yet *united* with us

19. Cheng-Tozun, "What Majority-World Missions Really Looks Like," *Christianity Today*, August 26, 2019.

20. Bryan, "Is the World's Next Mission Movement in Ethiopia?" *Christianity Today*, June 21, 2019.

21. Walls, *The Cross-cultural Process in Christian History*, 72–84.

through the work of Christ and his Spirit. As the Yale theologians Judith Gundry and Miroslav Volf have observed: "Pentecost, as the beginning of the new age of God's salvation, is not the reversion to the unity of cultural uniformity; it is an advance toward harmony in cultural diversity."[22] We are, Walls noted, now living in another Ephesians moment, a period of transition, when we must strive for unity in a culturally diverse church that is one in Christ.

CHALLENGES AND OPPORTUNITIES

Our Ephesians moment has created new challenges and exciting opportunities. There is the challenge of sharing resources. One mission strategist observes: "The Center of Christianity today has shifted south into Africa and Latin America" while "the center of material wealth and power remains in North America, Europe, and parts of Asia."[23] This difficulty requires wisdom, and a number of studies are now available to help the church think through ways to practice generosity so that "younger churches" are strengthened without creating debilitating generational dependence.[24] There is the challenge of theological disagreement. The majority church is, by-and-large, more conservative theologically and culturally than the Western church. This raises the possibility of learning from each other with the full recognition that the "Word of God did not originate with anyone single one of us" and that "we are not the only ones it has reached!"[25] Even with the emphasis being placed on indigenous theology, there are ways Christ may want to speak to each of us as we read and discuss the Scriptures together.[26] The rise

22. Gundry and Volf, *A Spacious Heart*, 9.

23. Lara-Braud, "The Role of North Americans in the Future of the Missionary Enterprise," 2–5.

24. Bonk, *Missions and Money* (2007); Corbett and Fikkert, *When Helping Hurts* (2012); Reese, *Roots and Remedies on the Dependency Syndrome in World Missions* (2010); Schwartz, *When Charity Destroy Dignity: Overcoming Unhealthy Dependency in the Christian Movement* (2007).

25. 1 Cor 14:36.

26. Jenkins, *The New Faces of Christianity* (2008); Jacobson, *Global Gospel*,

of World Christianity has heightened the church's awareness of the great social ills that exist in our world—poverty, disease, corruption, human trafficking, civil strife, the plight of refugees and the orphan crisis. How can the church find the delicate balance in the midst of these difficulties between evangelism and social responsibility? We have learned from our past failures of social action without proclamation (the liberal error) or proclamation without compassion (the fundamentalist error). How can we live out this call to work with both hands, that is to "proclaim the gospel" while also being good Samaritans to a world in need?[27] Persecution and martyrdom are modern-day realities, even while many people in the West remain oblivious to the suffering of Christians who live in difficult places.[28] How can the Western church learn to "weep with those who weep" even while we try to avoid creating a cult-of-martyrdom mentality? How can we, in this world of pain and suffering, also find ways to rejoice with those who rejoice? Much has been made of the 10/40 window and unreached people groups in the world today. How can the Western church strategically partner with the non-Western church to reach the unreached people of the world? As mission strategists Larry Pate and Lawrence Keyes have observed: "It is highly possible that [Western cooperation] with emerging missions (non-Western missions and missionaries) will prove to be the greatest single formula for evangelizing unreached people."[29] Since the church is growing so rapidly in the Global South, how can short-term mission trips (STMs) from the West be designed in such a way that they are mutually beneficial? A growing body of research is now showing that if STMs are planned well they can be used to build relationships, enhance

---

xv-xviii, 225–30.

27. "Evangelism and Social Responsibility: An Evangelical Commitment," Lausanne Occasional Paper 21.

28. Budde and Scott, *Witness of the Body: The Past, Present and Future of Christian Martyrdom* (2011); Marshall, *Persecuted: The Global Assault on Christians* (2013).

29. Pate with Keyes, "Emerging Missions in a Global Church."

cultural IQ, and enrich the spiritual lives of the Western church.[30] These and other important questions require careful consideration in the twenty-first century. However, if the twenty-first century is to become a new era of genuine partnerships, the Western church and the non-Western church will need to address some of these questions and challenges *together*. The Western church will need to move beyond its provincial attitudes, and listen to Christians in the non-Western world. As the Peruvian theologian Samuel Escobar wrote about our approach to missions in the twenty-first century:

> As we enter a new phase in the history of Christian mission, now with a truly global church, the time has come to reverse all kinds of provincialism that have characterized the relationship between churches new and old, rich and poor, North and South.

Although the Western church is part of the body of Christ and also has much to contribute, it will have to learn to listen. In the words of Paul Borthwick, who has offered sage counsel in his important 2012 work on the role of Western Christians in global mission, Western Christians will need to "tame the assertiveness" and start "listening to [their] non-Western Brothers and sisters."[31] These unanswered questions offer opportunities for us to learn from each other on our journey toward Christlikeness and in our quest to be more effective in global mission.

30. Corbett with Fikkert, *Helping Without Hurting in Short Term Missions: Participants Guide*; Howell, *Short-Term Mission: An Ethnography of Christian Travel Narrative and Experience*; Livermore, *Serving with Eyes Wide Open: Doing Short Term Missions with Cultural Intelligence.*

31. Borthwick, *Western Christians in Global Mission: What's the Role of the North American Church?* 119, 157–79. Borthwick's work contains helpful advice on how the Western church can change the way it approaches its engagement with the majority church.

SUMMARY AND CONCLUSION

The twentieth century has ushered in a new era of worldwide Christianity. More than 85 percent of the world's Christians are people of color—and the vast majority of those 85 percent live in Africa, Asia, Latin America, and Oceania. Historians and demographers are now studying in greater depth the growth of Christianity in the Global South and churning out insightful work on the dramatic changes occurring in the modern world. Christian missionaries, they have discovered, were not colonizers. They did take the gospel out to the world by utilizing some of the conveniences of colonialism, but the very people who rejected colonialism became committed followers of Christ and zealous propagators of the gospel. Missionaries did have an important role to play, but the good news spread in the main through global revivals and indigenous witness. Still, the task remains unfinished. Of the world's 7.5 billion people, 5 billion are unbelievers, and more than 3 billion remain culturally cut off from the gospel message. The Great Commission is not "the white man's burden"[32] or the unique call of any one nation. Racism and chauvinism in all its forms must be rejected in the new era of global mission. The gospel has transformed the people of the world into "one new person" united through the person of Christ. As the day of Southern Christianity is dawning, so is the era of partnerships. More churches are awakening to this new reality, even while challenges remain. The Western church does not have all the answers to these challenges and the next chapter remains to be written—*together*.

32. Escobar, *The New Global Mission*, 162.

Bibliography

"A Bleak Outlook Is Seen for Religion." *New York Times*, February 25, 1968.

Aaron, Sushil J. "Emulating Azariah: Evangelicals and Social Change in the Dangs." In *Evangelical Christianity and Democracy in Asia*, 87–130. Oxford: Oxford University Press, 2009.

Achebe, Chinua. *Things Fall Apart*. New York: Anchor, 1994.

Africa Inland Mission, Kenya Field Council Minutes. Richard Gehman Papers. Wheaton, IL: Billy Graham Center Archives.

"The African Church Planter: An Interview with Oscar Muriu." *Christianity Today*, April 2007. https://www.christianitytoday.com/pastors/2007/spring/3.96.html.

Aikman, David. *Jesus in Beijing: How Christianity Is Transforming China and Changing the Global Balance of Power*. Oxford: Monarch, 2007.

Anderson, Allan. *To the Ends of the Earth: Pentecostalism and the Transformation of World Christianity*. New York: Oxford, 2013.

———. *An Introduction to Pentecostalism: Global Charismatic Christianity*. Cambridge: Cambridge University Press, 2016.

Anderson, Gerald H., ed. *Biographical Dictionary of Christian Missions*. Grand Rapids: Eerdmans, 1998.

"Andrew F. Walls Centre for the Study of African and Asian Christianity." *International Bulletin of Missionary Research* 32, no. 2 (2008) 99.

Aritonang, Jan S., and Karel E. Steenbrink, eds. *A History of Christianity in Indonesia*. Leiden: Brill, 2008.

Arnold, David. *The Age of Discovery, 1400–1600*. Hoboken: Taylor and Francis, 2013.

Bacon, Daniel W. "From Faith to Faith: The Influence of the China Inland Mission on the Faith Missions Movement." D.Miss., Trinity Evangelical Divinity School, 1983.

Bailey, Sarah Pulliam. "How the Prosperity Gospel Is Sparking a Major Change in Predominantly Catholic Brazil." *The Washington Post*, October 31, 2017. https://www.washingtonpost.com/local/social-issues/forget-the-germans-this-is-where-the-protestant-reformation-debates-are-happening

-now/2017/10/29/7723af30-b807-11e7-be94-fabbof1e9ffb_story.html?utm_term=.18ecb6328d6c.

Barclay, Oliver, and Robert M. Horn. *From Cambridge to the World: 125 Years of Student Witness*. Leicester, UK: Inter-Varsity, 2002.

Barnett, Erik S. "Acceptance of Negro Missionaries from U.S.A. to Kenyan Field." Africa Inland Mission, Kenyan Field Report, April 16–21, 1951. Billy Graham Center Archives. AIM International, Collection 81. Wheaton, Illinois.

Barrett, David B. *Kenya Churches Handbook: The Development of Kenyan Christianity, 1483–1973*. Kisumu: Evangel House, 1973.

———. *Schism and Renewal in Africa: An Analysis of Six Thousand Contemporary Religious Movements*. Oxford: Oxford University Press, 1968.

———, ed. *World Christian Encyclopedia: A Comparative Survey of Churches and Religions in the Modern World, A.D. 1900–2000*. Oxford: Oxford University Press, 1982.

Barrett, David B., et al. *World Christian Encyclopedia: A Comparative Survey of Churches and Religions in the Modern World*. Oxford: Oxford University Press, 2001.

Barrett, David B., and Todd M. Johnson. *World Christian Trends AD 30–AD 2200: Interpreting the Annual Christian Megacensus*. Pasadena, CA: William Carey Library, 2001.

Bauman, Chad. *Pentecostals, Proselytization, and Anti-Christian Violence in Contemporary India*. Oxford: Oxford University Press, 2009.

Bauman, Chad M., and James Ponniah. "Christianity and Freedom in India: Colonialism, Communalism, Caste and Violence." In *Christianity and Freedom, Volume II: Contemporary Perspectives*, edited by Alan D. Hertzke and Timothy Samuel Shah, 222–53. Cambridge: Cambridge University Press, 2016.

Belloc, Hilaire. *Europe and the Faith*. New York: Paulist, 1920.

Beale, David O. *In Pursuit of Purity: American Fundamentalism Since 1850*. Greenville, SC: Unusual Publications, 1986.

Bebbington, Eileen, and Timothy Larsen. *A Patterned Life: Faith, History, and David Bebbington*. Eugene, OR: Wipf & Stock, 2014.

Bebbington, David W. *Baptists through the Centuries: A History of a Global People*. Waco, TX: Baylor University Press, 2018.

———. *Evangelicalism in Modern Britain: a history from the 1730s to the 1980s*. London: Unwin Hyman, 1988.

———. *Victorian Religious Revivals: Culture and Piety in Local and Global Contexts*. Oxford: Oxford University Press, 2012.

Becker, Amy Julia. "A Christian Response to Overpopulation." *Christianity Today*. May 25, 2011.

Bediako, Kwame. *Christianity in Africa: The Renewal of a Non-Western Religion*. Edinburgh: Edinburgh University Press, 1995.

Bell, James, and Neha Sahgal, eds. "Religion in Latin America: Widespread Change in a Historically Catholic Region." *Pew Research Center*. November 13, 2014. http://www.pewforum.org/2014/11/13/religion-in-latin-america/.

Bergen, Doris. *Twisted Cross: The German Christian Movement in the Third Reich*. Chapel Hill, NC: University of North Carolina Press, 1996.

Bird, Warren. "The World's Largest Churches: A Country-by-Country List of Global Megachurches." *Leadership Network*, September 2, 2018: http://leadnet.org/world/?/world.

Blakeslee, Virginia. "Revival News." *Inland Africa* XXXII, no. 158 (1950) 44.

Bonk, Jonathan. *Missions and Money: Affluence as a Western Missionary Problem—Revisited*. New Haven, CT: Overseas Mission Study Center, 2007.

Borthwick, Paul. *Western Christians in Global Mission: What's the Role of the North American Church*. Downers Grove, IL: IVP, 2012.

Broward, Josh. "Think Big, Think Small: Partnership as a Revolution in Global Missions." *Evangelical Missions Quarterly* 51, no. 2 (2015) 180–89.

Bosch, David. *Transforming Mission: Paradigm Shifts in Theology of Missions*. Maryknoll, NY: Orbis, 1992.

Bowler, Kate. *Blessed: A History of the Prosperity Gospel*. New York: Oxford University Press, 2013.

Brereton, Virginia Lieson. *Training God's Army: The American Bible School, 1880–1940*. Bloomington, IN: Indiana University Press, 1990.

Brouwer, Steve, Paul Gifford, and Susan D. Rose. *Exporting the American Gospel: Global Christian Fundamentalism*. London: Routledge, 1997.

Brown, Callum G. *The Death of Christian Britain: Understanding Secularisation, 1800–2000*. London: Routledge, 2010.

Bryan, Jack. "Is the World's Next Mission Movement in Ethiopia?" *Christianity Today*, June 21, 2019. https://www.christianitytoday.com/ct/2019/july-august/ethiopia-missions.html.

Budde, Michael L., and Karen Scott. *Witness of the Body: The Past, Present and Future of Christian Martyrdom*. Grand Rapids: Eerdmans, 2011.

Bundy, David. "Early Asian and East African Christianities." In *The Cambridge History of Christianity, Vol. 2, Constantine to c. 600*, edited by Augustine Casiday and Frderick W. Norris, 118–48. Cambridge: Cambridge University Press, 2007.

Burton, Keith Augustus. *The Blessing of Africa: The Bible and African Christianity*. Downers Grove, IL: IVP Academic, 2007.

Cabrita, Joel, et al. *Relocating World Christianity: Interdisciplinary Studies in Universal and Local Expression of the Christian Faith*. Leiden: Brill, 2017.

Cambell, Ian. "Pan-Africanism." In *A Concise Oxford Dictionary of Politics and International Relations*, edited by Garrett W. Brown, Ian McLean, and Alistair McMillan. Oxford: Oxford University Press, 2018. Online.

Cambridge Centre for Christianity Worldwide, Minutes of the Meeting of Trustees, Minute Book 1887–1939. Cambridge, UK.

Carey, William. *An Enquiry into the Obligation of the Christians to Use Means for the Conversion of the Heathen*. Reprinted in facsimile from the edition of MDCCXCII. London: Hodder & Stoughton, 1892.

Carpenter, Joel A. *Christian Higher Education: A Global Reconnaissance*. Grand Rapids: Eerdmans, 2014.

———. "'To be agents of life-giving transformation:' Christian Higher Education in Africa." Day Lecture, Annual Meeting of the Yale-Edinburgh Group. New Haven, CT: Yale Divinity School, June 28, 2019 (unpublished paper).

Carpenter, Joel A., and Wibert R. Shenk, eds. *Earthen Vessels: American Evangelicals and Foreign Missions, 1880–1990*. Grand Rapids: Eerdmans, 1990.

Carter, Humphrey. *The Inklings: C. S. Lewis, J. R. R. Tolkien, C. Williams and Their Friends*. London: George Allen & Unwin, 1978.

"Celebrating 50 Years of Global Christian Research." South Hamilton, MA: Gordon-Conwell Theological Seminary, 2015. http://www.gordonconwell.edu/ockenga/research/documents/50thbookletFINAL.pdf.

Cheng-Tozun, Dorcas. "What Majority-World Missions Really Looks Like." *Christianity Today*, August 26, 2019. https://www.christianitytoday.com/women/2019/august/what-majority-world-missions-really-looks-like.html.

Chester, C. H. "Church Union in Kenya." *The Missionary* 39, no. 5 (1906) 32.

Chestnut, R. Andrews. *Born Again in Brazil: The Pentecostal Boom and the Pathogens of Poverty*. New Brunswick, NJ: Rutgers University Press, 1997.

Church, J. E. *Quest for the Highest: An Autobiographical Account of the East African Revival*. Exeter, UK: Paternoster, 1981.

Coleman, Simon. "Christianity in Western Europe: Mission Fields, Old and New?" In *Introducing World Christianity*, edited by Charles E. Farhadian, 65–76. Oxford: Wiley-Blackwell, 2012.

Columbus, Christopher. *The Log of Christopher Columbus*. Translated by Robert H. Fuson. Camden, ME: International Marine Publishing, 1992.

Conforti, Joseph. "Jonathan Edwards' Most Popular Work: 'The Life of David Brainerd' and Nineteenth-Century Evangelical Culture." *Church History: Studies in Christianity and Culture* 54, no. 2 (1985) 188–201.

Coote, Robert T. "'AD 2000' and the '10/40 Window': A Preliminary Assessment." *International Bulletin of Missionary Research* 24, no. 4 (2000) 160–66.

Corbett, Steve, and Brian Fikkert. *When Helping Hurts: How to Alleviate Poverty without Hurting the Poor—and Yourself*. Chicago: Moody, 2009.

———. *Helping without Hurting in Short Term Missions: Participants Guide*. Chicago: Moody, 2014.

Cross, F. L. and E. A. Livingstone, eds. *Dictionary of the Christian Church*. Peabody, MA: Hendrickson, 2007.

Dados, Nour, and Raewn Connell. "The Global South." *Contexts* 11, no. 1 (2012) 12–13.

"Dura Europos." *Dictionary of the Christian Church*, edited by F. L. Cross and E. A. Livingstone, 516–17. Oxford: Oxford University Press, 1997.

Daughrity, Dyron B. *Bishop Stephen Neill: From Edinburgh to South India*. New York: Lang, 2008.

———. *The Changing Face of World Christianity: The Global History of a Borderless Religion*. New York: Lang, 2010.

———. *To Whom Does Christianity Belong? Critical Issues in World Christianity*. Minneapolis, MN: Fortress, 2015.

Daughrity, Dyron B., and Jesudas M. Athyal. *Understanding World Christianity: India*. Minneapolis, MN: Fortress, 2016.

Dinesen, Isak. *Out of Africa*. New York: Modern Library, 1992.

De Graft, J. C. *Muntu*. London: Heinemann Educational, 1982.

De Gruchy, Steve. "Religion and Racism: Struggles around Segregation, 'Jim Crow' and Apartheid." In *The Cambridge History of Christianity: Volume 9: World Christianities, c. 1914–c. 2000*, edited by Hugh McLeod, 385–400. Cambridge: Cambridge University Press, 2006.

Devitt, Edith. *On the Edge of the Rift Valley*. Langley, BC: University Printers, 1992.

Dictionary of African Christian Biography. New Haven, CT: Center for Global Christianity & Mission, 1998.

Dow, Philip E. *"School in the Clouds": The Rift Valley Academy Story*. Pasadena, CA: William Carey Library, 2003.

Du Bois, W. E. B. "American Negroes and Africa's Rise to Freedom." *National Guardian*. February 13, 1961. In *The World and Africa*, edited by Henry Louis Gates, Jr., 168–69. Oxford: Oxford University Press, 2007.

———. *Du Bois' Writings*. New York: The American Library, 1968.

Edwards, Wendy J. Deichmann. "Forging an Ideology for American Missions: Josiah Strong and Manifest Destiny." In *North American Foreign Missions, 1810–1914*, 163–91. Grand Rapids: Eerdmans, 2004.

Escobar, Samuel. *The New Global Mission: The Gospel from Everywhere to Everyone*. Downers Grove, IL: InterVarsity, 2003.

Esterline, David. "From Western Church to World Christianity: Developments in Theological Education in the Ecumenical Movement." In *Handbook of Theological Education in World Christianity*, edited by David Werner, et al., 13–22. Oxford: Regnum, 2010.

Evans, Richard. *In Defense of History*. New York: Norton, 2000.

"Evangelism and Social Responsibility: An Evangelical Commitment." Lausanne Occasional Papers 21, Lausanne Committee for World Evangelism, 1982. https://www.lausanne.org/content/lop/lop-21.

Farhadian, Charles E. *Introducing World Christianity*. Oxford: Wiley-Blackwell, 2012.

Fihlani, Pumza. "Why Some African Governments Are Clamping Down on Churches." *BBC News*, February 7, 2016. https://www.bbc.com/news/world-africa-35362567.

Freston, Paul. "Contours of Latin American Pentecostalism." In *Christianity Reborn: The Global Expansion of Evangelicalism in the Twentieth Century*, edited by Donald Lewis, 221–70. Grand Rapids: Eerdmans, 2004.

———. "'Neo-Pentecostalism' in Brazil: Problems of Definition and the Struggle for Hegemony." *Archives De Sciences Sociales Des Religions* 44, no. 105 (1999) 145–62.

Frykenberg, R. E. *Christianity in India: From Beginnings to the Present*. Oxford: Oxford University Press, 2008.

———. "India." In *A World History of Christianity*, edited by Adrian Hastings, 147–91. Grand Rapids: Eerdmans, 1999.

Gatũ, John G. *Fan into Flame: An Autobiography*. Nairobi: Moran, 2016.

Gibson, David. "The Story behind Pope Francis' Election." *USA Today*, March 16, 2013. https://eu.usatoday.com/story/news/world/2013/03/16/pope-francis-election-conclave/1992797/.

Githii, David Muhia. *The East African Revival Movement and the Presbyterian Church of East Africa*. Fuller Theological Seminary: Th.M. Thesis, 1992.

"Global Survey on Theological Education: Summary of Main Findings." Busan, Indonesia: WCC, 2013.

"Globalization and the Gospel: Rethinking Mission in the Contemporary World." Luasanne Occasional Paper 30, Pattaya, Thailand (2004). https://www.lausanne.org/content/globalization-gospel-rethinking-mission-contemporary-world-lop-30.

González, Ondina E., and Justo L. González. *Christianity in Latin America*. Cambridge: Cambridge University Press, 2008.

Gonsalves, Kelly. "The 'long, hot summer of 1967.'" *The Week*, August 2, 1997. http://theweek.com/captured/712838/long-hot-summer-1967.

Goodpasture, H. McKennie. "Dennis, James Shephard." In *Biographical Dictionary of Christian Missions*, edited by Gerald H. Anderson, 176. New York: Macmillan, 1998.

Graham, Billy. *Christianity vs. Communism*. Minneapolis, MN: Billy Graham Association, 1951.

Greenman, Jeffery P., and Gene L. Green. "The Priority of Leadership Training in Global Mission." *Evangelical Missions Quarterly* 50, no. 2 (2015) 180–89.

Gregorious, and Henry Davis. *St. Gregory the Great: Pastoral Care*. New York: Newman, 1978.

Groves, C. P. *The Planting of Christianity in Africa, Volume IV, 1914–1954*. London: Lutterworth, 1958.

Gundry, Judith M., and Miroslav Volf. *A Spacious Heart: Essays on Identity and Belonging*. Harrisburg, PA: Trinity, 1997.

Gundry, S. N. "Death of God Theology." In *Evangelical Dictionary of Theology*, edited by Walter A. Elwell, 301–2. Grand Rapids: Eerdmans, 1984.

Hardage, Jeanette. *Mary Slessor—Everybody's Mother: The Era and Impact of a Victorian Missionary*. Eugene, OR: Wipf & Stock, 2008.

Harder, Ben. "The Student Volunteer Movement for Foreign Missions and Its Contribution to Overall Missionary Service." *Christian Higher Education* 10, no. 2 (2011) 140–54.

Harper, Susan Billington. "Azariah, Samuel Vedanayagam." In *Biographical Dictionary of Christian Missions*, edited by Gerald H. Anderson, 35–36. New York: Macmillan, 1998.

———. *In the Shadow of the Mahatma: Bishop V. S. Azariah and the Travails of Christianity in British India.* Grand Rapids: Eerdmans, 2000.

Hartch, Todd. *The Rebirth of Latin American Christianity.* Oxford: Oxford University Press, 2014.

———. *Understanding World Christianity: Mexico.* Minneapolis, MN: Fortress, 2019.

Hastings, Adrian. *The Church in Africa, 1450–1950.* Oxford: Oxford University Press, 1994.

———. *A History of Christianity in Africa, 1950–1975.* Cambridge: Cambridge University Press, 1979.

Hatch, Nathan. *The Democratization of American Christianity.* New Haven, CT: Yale, 1991.

Hattaway, Paul. "A Captivating Vision: Why Chinese House Churches May Just End Up Fulfilling the Great Commission." *Christianity Today*, April 1, 2004.

Heale, Michael J. *The Sixties in America: History, Politics and Protest.* Edinburgh: Edinburgh University Press, 2004.

Hendricks, Barbara, and C. René Padilla. "Mission in the 1990s: Two Views." *International Bulletin of Missionary Research* 13, no. 4 (1989) 146–52.

Henman, Philip S. "Power?" *Inland Africa*, British edition, XLI, no. 32 (April 1959) 1.

Herder, Ben. "The Student Volunteer Movement for Foreign Missions and Its Contribution to 20th Century Missions." *Missiology: An International Review* 8, no. 2 (1980) 141–54.

Herrman, Cassandra. "An African's Message for America." *New York Times.* January 5, 2015.

Hilliard, David. "Australia and the Pacific." *A World History of Christianity*, edited by Adrian Hastings, 508–35. Grand Rapids: Eerdmans, 1999.

Hollinger, David A. *After Cloven Tongues of Fire: Protestant Liberalism in Modern American History.* Princeton: Princeton University Press, 2013.

Honer, Mary Anderson. *The Downing Legacy: Six Decades at Rift Valley Academy.* Bloomington, IN: iUniverse, 2010.

Howell, Brian. *Short-Term Mission: An Ethnography of Christian Travel Narrative and Experience.* Downers Grove, IL: IVP Academic, 2012.

Hughes, Hugh Price. *Methodist Times* 18. January 2, 1902.

Hunt, Everett N. Jr. "Nevius, John Livingstone." In *Biographical Dictionary of Christian Missions*, edited by Gerald H. Anderson, 490. New York: Macmillan, 1998.

Hsu, Becky, et al. "Estimating the Religious Composition of All Nations: An Empirical Assessment of the World Christian Database." *Journal for the Scientific Study of Religion* 47, no. 4 (2008) 678–93.

Hutchinson, Mark, and John Wolffe. *A Short History of Global Evangelicalism.* Cambridge: Cambridge University Press, 2012.

"Indonesia: Turmoil Amid Revival." *Christianity Today* 12, no. 6, December 22, 1967.

"Indonesia–Location, Size and Extent." *National Encyclopedia.* https://www.nationsencyclopedia.com/Asia-and-Oceania/Indonesia-LOCATION-SIZE-AND-EXTENT.html.

"Is God Dead?" *Time* (Magazine) Cover, April 4, 1966.

"Islands See Miracles." *Christian Life*, November 1967.

Jacobson, Douglas. *Global Gospel: An Introduction to Christianity on Five Continents.* Grand Rapids: Baker Academic, 2015.

———. *The World's Christians: Who They Are, Where They Are, and How They Got There.* Oxford: Wiley-Blackwell, 2011.

Jenkins, Philip. "After the Next Christendom." *International Bulletin of Missionary Research* 28, no. 1 (2004) 20–22.

———. *God's Continent: Christianity, Islam and Europe's Religious Crisis.* Oxford: Oxford University Press, 2007.

———. *The Lost History of Christianity: The Thousand-Year Golden Age of the Church in the Middle East, Africa and Asia—and How It Died.* New York: HarperCollins, 2008.

———. *The New Faces of Christianity: Believing the Bible in the Global South.* Oxford: Oxford University Press, 2006.

———. *The Next Christendom: The Coming of Global Christianity.* Oxford: Oxford University Press, 2002.

Jenkins, Simon. "England's Churches Can Survive—but the Religion Will Have to Go." *The Guardian*, October 22, 2015.

Joe Edward Church Papers. Cambridge Centre for Christianity Worldwide. Cambridge, UK. https://www.cccw.cam.ac.uk/?archives=church-john-edward-joe.

Johnson, Todd M. "David B. Barrett: Missionary Statistician." *International Bulletin of Missionary Research* 36, no. 1 (2012) 30–32.

Johnson, Todd M., and Kenneth Ross, eds. *Atlas of Global Christianity, 1910–2010.* Edinburgh: Edinburgh University Press, 2009.

Johnson, Todd M., and Gina Zurlow eds. *World Christian Encyclopedia.* Edinburgh: Edinburgh University Press, 2020.

Johnstone, Patrick. *The Church Is Bigger Than You Think: The Unfinished Task of World Evangelisation.* Fearn, UK: Christian Focus, 2005.

Johnstone, Patrick, and Jason Mandryk. *Operation World: 21st Century Edition.* Carlisle, UK: Paternoster, 2001.

Jones, Larry B. "The Problem of Power in Ministry Relationships." *Evangelical Missions Quarterly* 5, no. 4 (2009) 404–10.

Jones, Tracy K. Jr. "History's Lessons for Tomorrow's Mission." *International Bulletin of Missionary Research* 10, no. 2 (1986) 50–53.

The Joshua Project. https://joshuaproject.net.

Keen, Benjamin, trans. and ed. *Latin American Civilization: History and Society, 1492–Present*. Boulder, CO: Westview, 1991.

Keller, Timothy. Twitter post. February 6, 2017, 9:04 a.m. https://twitter.com/timkellernyc/status/828620265017974784.

Kendi, Ibram X. *Stamped from the Beginning: The Definitive History of Racist Ideas in America*. New York: Bold Type Books, 2016.

Kim, Sebastian, and Kirsteen Kim. *Christianity as a World Religion*. London: Continuum, 2008.

———. *A History of Christianity in Korea*. Cambridge: Cambridge University Press, 2015.

Kingsolver, Barbara. *The Poisonwood Bible*. New York: HarperCollins, 1998.

Koch, Kurt E. *The Revival in Indonesia*. Grand Rapids: Kregel, 1972.

———. *Victory through Persecution*. Grand Rapids: Kregel, 1972.

———. *Wine of God: Revival in Indonesia, Formosa, Solomon Islands, and South India*. Grand Rapids: Christian Evangelism, 1974.

Kollman, Paul V., and Cynthia Toms Smedley. *Understanding World Christianity: Eastern Africa*. Minneapolis, MN: Fortress, 2015.

"Korea." *The Missionary* 41, no. 1 (1908) 36.

Kronk, Rick. "Successful Partnership: A Case Study." *Evangelical Missions Quarterly* 46, no. 2 (2010) 180–89.

Kuzmic, Peter. "Christianity in Eastern Europe: A Story of Pain, Glory, Persecution and Freedom." In *Introducing World Christianity*, edited by Charles E. Farhadian, 77–79. Oxford: Wiley-Blackwell, 2012.

Kwong-Chan, Kim. *Understanding World Christianity: China*. Minneapolis, MN: Fortress, 2019.

Lacy, Creighton. "Toward a Post-Denominational World Church." In *Beyond Establishment: Protestant Identity in a Post-Protestant Age*, edited by Jackson W. Carroll and Wade Clark Roof, 327–42. Louisville, KY: John Knox, 1993.

Lara-Braud, Jorge. "The Role of North Americans in the Future of the Missionary Enterprise." *International Bulletin of Missionary Research* 7, no. 1 (1983) 2–5.

Lee, Timothy S. *Born Again: Evangelicalism in Korea*. Honolulu: University of Hawaii Press, 2016.

Lewis, R. W. "Clarifying the Remaining Frontier Mission Task." *International Journal of Frontier Mission* 35, no. 4 (2018) 154–68.

Littlefield, Christina. *Chosen Nations: Pursuit of the Kingdom of God and Its Influence on Democratic Values in Late Nineteenth Century Britain and the United States*. Minneapolis, MN: Fortress, 2013.

Livermore, David. *Serving with Eyes Wide Open: Doing Short Term Missions with Cultural Intelligence*. Grand Rapids: Baker, 2012.

Livingstone, David. Speech "Delivered before the University of Cambridge, in the Senate-House, on Friday, 4th December 1857." In *Dr Livingstone's Cambridge Lectures: Together with a Prefatory Note by the Rev. Professor Sedgwick*, edited by William Monk, 1–24. Cambridge: Cambridge University Press, 2009.

Lloyd, Margaret. "Echoes of Revival." *Inland Africa* XXXIII, no. 159 (1950) 57.

Lugo, Luis, and Alan Cooperman. "'Nones' on the Rise." *Pew Research Center*, October 9, 2012. http://www.pewforum.org/2012/10/09/nones-on-the-rise/.

Lyall, Leslie T. *John Sung*. London: China Inland Mission, 1955.

MacCulloch, Dairmaid. *Christianity: The First Three Thousand Years*. New York: Viking, 2010.

MacMaster, R. K., and D. R. Jacobs. *A Gentle Wind of God: The Influence of the East Africa Revival*. Scottdale, PA: Herald, 2006.

Marsden, George. "Christianity and Cultures: Transforming Niebuhr's Categories." *Insights: The Faculty Journal of Austin Seminary* (Fall 1999) 4–15.

———. *Jonathan Edwards: A Life*. New Haven, CT: Yale University Press, 2003.

Marshall, Paul. *Persecuted: The Global Assault on Christians*. Nashville, TN: Thomas Nelson, 2013.

Martyn, John R. C. *Henry Martyn (1781–1812) Scholar and Missionary to India and Persia*. Lewistown, NY: Mellen, 1999.

Masci, David. "Why Has Pentecostalism Grown So Dramatically in Latin America?" *Pew Research Center*. November 14, 2014. http://www.pewresearch.org/fact-tank/2014/11/14/why-has-pentecostalism-grown-so-dramatically-in-latin-america/.

Mariz, Cecília, and Eloísa Martín. "Christianity in South America, 1910–2010." In *Atlas of Global Christianity, 1910–2010*, edited by Todd M. Johnson and Kenneth R. Ross, 186–87. Edinburgh: Edinburgh University Press, 2009.

Massam, Katharine. "Christian Churches in Australia, New Zealand and the Pacific, 1914–1970." In *The Cambridge History of World Christianity, Vol. 9, World Christianities, 1914–2000*, edited by Hugh McLeod, 252–61. Cambridge: Cambridge University Press, 2014.

McCracken, Bret. "Scorsese's 'Silence' Asks What It Really Costs to Follow Jesus: Martin Scorsese adapts Shusaku Endo's acclaimed novel about Faith, Mission and Suffering." *Christianity Today*, December 16, 2016. https://www.christianitytoday.com/ct/2016/december-web-only/silence-whispers-loudly-of-christs-love.html.

McGavran, Donald Anderson. *The Bridges of God: A Study in the Strategy of Missions*. London: World Dominion, 1955.

McKenzie, Robert Tracy. "The Most Famous Metaphor of American Exceptionalism Is a Warning, Not a Boast." *Christianity Today*, November 21, 2018. https://www.christianitytoday.com/ct/2018/november-web-only/most-famous-metaphor-of-american-exceptionalism-is-warning-.html.

McWilliams, John C. *The 1960s Cultural Revolution*. Westport, CT: Greenwood, 2002.

Meredith, Martin. *The Fate of Africa: From the Hopes of Freedom to the Heart of Despair: A History of 50 Years of Independence*. New York: Public Affairs, 2005.

Minkema, Kenneth P. "David Brainerd (1718–1747)." In *Biographical Dictionary of Christian Missions*, edited by Gerald H. Anderson, 84–85. New York: Macmillan, 1998.

"Mission Researcher David Barrett Dies." *Baptist Press*, August 8, 2011. http://www.bpnews.net/35901/missions-researcher-david-barrett-dies.

Moffett, Samuel Hugh. *A History of Christianity in Asia*. Maryknoll, NY: Orbis, 2005.

Mott, John R. *The Evangelization of the World in This Generation*. New York: Student Volunteer Movement for Foreign Missions, 1900.

Moll, Rob. "Missions Incredible." *Christianity Today*, March 1, 2006. https://www.christianitytoday.com/ct/2006/march/16.28.html.

Moyn, Samuel. *Christian Human Rights*. Philadelphia: University of Pennsylvania Press, 2015.

Mubulaki, Kangwa. "Diversified Theological Education: Genesis, Development, and Ecumenical Potential of Theological Education by Extension." In *Handbook of Theological Education in World Christianity: Theological Perspectives, Regional Surveys, Ecumenical Trends*, edited by Dietrich Werner, et al., 251–62. Oxford: Regnum, 2010.

Muriu, Oscar. "The Global Church." Address given at Urbana. InterVarsity, 2006. https://vimeo.com/69504380.

Murray, Lorraine. "Christ the Redeemer Statue, Mount Corcovado, Brazil." *Encyclopedia Britannica*. https://www.britannica.com/topic/Christ-the-Redeemer.

"Nairobi Communiqué and Commitment." October 26, 2013. https://www.gafcon.org/news/nairobi-communique-and-commitment.

Niebuhr, Gustav. "As the Old-Line Anglican Churches Wilt, Those in Africa Flower Profusely." *The New York Times*, August 2, 1998. https://www.nytimes.com/1998/08/02/world/as-the-old-line-anglican-churches-wilt-those-in-africa-flower-profusely.html.

Niebuhr, Richard H. *Christ and Culture*. New York: Harper, 1951.

Neill, Stephen. *A History of Christian Missions*. New York: Pelican, 1964.

———. *The Unfinished Task*. London: Edinburgh House, 1957.

Neely, Alan. "Moon, Charlotte ('Lottie') Diggs (1840–1912)." In *Dictionary of Christian Missions*, edited by Gerald H. Anderson, 471. New York: Macmillan, 1998.

———. "Samuel Austin Moffett (1864–1939)." In *Biographical Dictionary of Christian Missions*, 465. New York: Macmillan, 1998.

Nevius, John L. *Methods of Mission Work*. New York: Foreign Mission Library, 1896.

Njogu, Kimani. "Gatũ, John (1925–)." In *Dictionary of African Biography*, edited by Henry Louis Gates, Jr., 430–32. Oxford: Oxford University Press, 2011.

Nolde, Otto Frederick, ed. *Toward World-Wide Christianity*. New York: Harper, 1946.

Noll, Mark A. *From Every Tribe and Nation: A Historian's Discovery of the Global Church*. Grand Rapids: Baker Academic, 2014.

———. *The New Shape of World Christianity: How American Experience Reflects Global Faith*. Downers Grove, IL: InterVarsity, 2009.

———. *The Old Religion in a New World: The History of North American Christianity*. Grand Rapids: Eerdmans, 2002.

———. *The Rise of Evangelicalism: The Age of Edwards, Whitfield and the Wesleys*. Downers Grove, IL: IVP Academic, 2003.

———. *The Scandal of the Evangelical Mind*. Grand Rapids: Eerdmans, 1994.

———. "Turning the World Upside Down: The Coming of Global Christianity." *Books & Culture*, March/April 2012. https://www.booksandculture.com/articles/2002/marapr/16.32.html?paging=off.

"O Come All Ye Faithful." *The Economist*, November 1, 2007. https://www.economist.com/special-report/2007/11/01/o-come-all-ye-faithful.

Oden, Thomas C. *How Africa Shaped the Christian Mind: Rediscovering the African Seedbed of Western Christianity*. Downers Grove, IL: InterVarsity Press, 2010.

Oliver, Roland. *In the Realms of Gold: Pioneering in African History*. London: Cass, 1977.

Orr, J. Edwin. *Evangelical Awakenings in Eastern Asia*. Minneapolis, MN: Bethany House, 1975.

———. *Evangelical Awakenings in Southern Asia*. Minneapolis, MN: Bethany House, 1975.

Ostling, Richard and Alistair Matheson. "Counting Every Soul on Earth: Miracle from Nairobi: The First Census of All Religions." *Time*. May 2, 1982.

Pachau, Lalsangkima. *World Christianity: A Historical and Theological Introduction*. Nashville: Abingdon, 2015.

Pate, Larry D. *From Every People: A Handbook of Two-Thirds World Missions with Directory, History and Analysis*. Monrovia, CA: MARC, 1989.

Pate, Larry D., with Lawrence E. Keyes, "Emerging Missions in a Global Church." *International Bulletin of Missionary Research* 10, no. 4 (1986) 156–61.

"Pentecostalism in Brazil: From Modesty to Ostentation." *The Economist*. January 23, 2016. https://www.economist.com/international/2016/01/23/from-modesty-to-ostentation.

Persuad, Trevor. "Douglas Moses Carew, 1956–2012." *Dictionary of African Christian Biography* (2016). https://dacb.org/stories/kenya/carew-douglas/.

Peterson, Derek R. *Ethnic Patriotism and the East African Revival: A History of Dissent, 1935–1972*. Cambridge: Cambridge University Press, 2012.

Piper, John. *Bloodlines: Race, Cross and the Christian*. Wheaton, IL: Crossway, 2011.

———. *Let the Nations Be Glad: The Supremacy of God in Missions*. Nottingham, UK: InterVarsity, 2010.

Plowman, Edward E. "Demythologizing Indonesia's Revival." *Christianity Today* 17, no. 11. March 2, 1973.

Pollock, John C. *A Cambridge Movement*. London: Marshall, Morgan and Scott, 1953.

Porter, Andrew. *Religion Versus Empire? British Overseas Protestant Missionaries and Overseas Expansion, 1700–1914*. Manchester: Manchester University Press, 2004.

Porter, Andrew N. "War, Colonialism and the British Experience: The Redefinition of Christian Missionary Policy, 1938–1952." *Kirthliche Zeitgeschichte* 5, no. 2 (1992) 269–288.

Potterfield, Amanda. *Mary Lyon and the Mount Holyoke Missionaries*. New York: Oxford University Press, 1997.

Priest, Robert J., Douglas Wilson, and Adelle Johnson. "U.S. Mega-churches and New Patterns of Global Mission." *International Bulletin of Missionary Research* 34, no. 2 (2010) 97–103.

Preston, J. Fairman. "The Awakening of Mopko." *The Missionary* 39, no. 1 (1906) 32.

Putney, Clifford, and Paul T. Burlin. *The Role of the American Board in the World: Bicentennial Reflections on the Organization's Missionary Work, 1810–2010*. Eugene, OR: Wipf & Stock, 2012.

Randall, Ian. *The Cambridge Seventy: A Missionary Movement in Twentieth-Century Britain*. Cambridge, UK: Cambridge Centre for Christianity Worldwide, 2016.

———. *Cambridge Students and Christianity Worldwide: Insights from the 1960s*. Cambridge: Cambridge Centre for Christianity Worldwide, 2019.

Rattansi, Ali. *Racism: A Very Short Introduction*. Oxford: Oxford University Press, 2007.

Reese, Robert. "John Gatũ and the Moratorium on Missionaries." *Missiology: An International Review* 43, no. 3 (2014) 245–56.

———. *Roots and Remedies on the Dependency Syndrome in World Missions*. Pasadena, CA: William Carey Library, 2010.

"Religion in Latin America: Pentecostalism." *Pew Research Center*. November 13, 2014. http://www.pewforum.org/2014/11/13/chapter-4-pentecostalism/.

Robert, Dana. *American Women in Mission: The Modern Era, 1792–1992*. Mason, GA: Mercer University Press, 1998.

———. *Christian Mission: How Christianity Became a World Religion*. Malden, MA: Wiley-Blackwell, 2009.

———. *Faithful Friendships: Embracing Diversity in Christian Community*. Grand Rapids: Eerdmans, 2019.

———. "Global Friendship as Incarnational Mission Practice." *International Bulletin of Missionary Research* 39, no. 4 (2015) 180–84.

———. *Gospel Bearers, Gender Barriers: Missionary Women in the Twentieth Century*. Maryknoll, NY: Orbis, 2002.

———. "The Influence of American Missionary Women on the World Back Home." *Religion and American Culture: A Journal of Interpretation* 12, no. 1 (2012) 59–89.

———. "Naming 'World Christianity': Historical and Personal Perspectives on the Yale-Edinburgh Conference in World Christianity and Mission History." *International Bulletin of Missionary Research*, December 30, 2019, 1–18.

———. *Occupy Until I Come: A. T. Pierson and the Evangelization of the World*. Grand Rapids: Eerdmans, 2003.

———. "Shifting Southward." *International Bulletin of Missionary Research* 24, no. 2 (2000) 55–58.

Robert, Dana, ed. *Converting Colonialism: Visions and Reality in Missions History, 1706–1914*. Grand Rapids: Eerdmans, 2008.

Roberts, Gene. "Detroit Riots Reported Curbed After Tanks Fight Day Snipers: Death Toll at 35." *New York Times*, July 27, 1967.

"Record Numbers of Visitors and Worshippers Flock to England's Cathedrals." The Church of England Research and Statistics, November 26, 2010. https://www.churchofengland.org/more/media-centre/news/record-numbers-visitors-and-worshippers-flock-englands-cathedrals.

Ross, Kathy. "The Theology of Partnership." *International Bulletin of Missionary Research* 34, no. 3 (2010) 145–49.

Ross, Kenneth R., et al. *Christianity in South and Central Asia*. Edinburgh: Edinburgh University Press, 2019.

"Rudyard Kipling (1965–1936)." In *The Oxford Companion to English Literature*, edited by Dinah Birch, ?–?. Oxford: Oxford University Press, 2006.

"Rwanda Church Closures: Pastors Arrested for Defying Order." *BBC News*. March 6, 2018. https://www.bbc.com/news/world-africa-43301517.

Saad, Lydia. "Catholics' Church Attendance Resumes Downward Slide." *Gallup*, April 9, 2018. https://news.gallup.com/poll/232226/church-attendance-among-catholics-resumes-downward-slide.aspx.

Samuel, Vinay, and Chris Sugden. "Mission Agencies as Multinationals." *International Bulletion of Missionary Research* 7, no. 4 (1999) 152–55.

Sandgren, David P. *Christianity and the Kikuyu: Religious Divisions and Social Conflict*. New York: Lang, 2000.

Sands, Kirkley. "Christianity in the Caribbean, 1910–2010." In *Atlas of Global Christianity, 1910–2010*, edited by Todd M. Johnson and Kenneth R. Ross, 178–81. Edinburgh: Edinburgh University Press, 2009.

Sanneh, Lamin. *Beyond Jihad: The Pacifist Tradition in West African Islam*. New York: Oxford, 2016.

———. *Summoned from the Margin: Homecoming of An African*. Grand Rapids: Eerdmans, 2012.

———. *Translating the Message: The Missionary Impact on Culture*. Maryknoll, NY: Orbis, 1989.

———. *Whose Religion Is Christianity?* Grand Rapids: Eerdmans, 2003.

Sanneh, Lamin, and Joel Carpenter, eds. *The Changing Face of Christianity: Africa, the West, and the World.* New York: Oxford University Press, 2005.

Santoso, Aboeprijadi, and Gerry van Klinken. "Genocide Finally Enters Public Discourse: The International People's Tribunal 1965." *Journal of Genocide Research* 19, no. 4 (2017) 594–608.

Scherer, James A. *Missionary, Go Home!* Englewood Cliffs, NJ: Prentice-Hall, 1964.

Schwartz, Glenn. *When Charity Destroys Dignity: Overcoming Unhealthy Dependency in the Christian Movement.* Lancaster, PA: World Missions Associates, 2007.

Sciolino, Elaine. "Europeans Fast Falling Away from the Church." *New York Times*, April 19, 2005.

Schuster, Kathleen. "6 Facts about Catholic and Protestant Influence in Germany." *Deutsch Welle*, March 23, 2018.

Shaw, Ian. "John Stott and the Langham Scholarship Programme." In *Reflection on and Equipping for Christian Mission*, edited by Stephen Bevans, et al., 308–326. Oxford: Regnum, 2015.

Shaw, Mark. *Global Awakening: How 20th-Century Revivals Triggered a Christian Revolution.* Downers Grove, IL: InterVarsity, 2010.

———. *The Kingdom of God in Africa: A Short History of African Christianity.* Grand Rapids: Baker, 1996.

Shellnutt, Kate. "Why Mission Experts Are Redefining 'Unreached People Groups.'" *Christianity Today*, April 22, 2019. https://www.christianitytoday.com/ct/2019/may/redefining-unreached-people-groups-frontier-unengaged-missi.html.

Sherwood, Harriet. "'Christianity as Default Is Gone': The Rise of a Non-Christian Europe." *The Guardian*, March 21, 2018.

———. "More Than Half of UK Population Has No Religion, Finds a Survey." *The Guardian*, September 4, 2017.

Skrentny, John. "The Effect of the Cold War on African-American Civil Rights: America and the World Audience, 1945–1968." *Theory and Society* 27, vol. 2 (1998) 237–85.

Smail, John R. W. "Descent into Chaos." In *Pacific Century: The Emergence of Modern Pacific Asia*, edited by Mark Borthwick. Boulder, CO: Westview, 2020.

Smith, Christian Stephen. *American Evangelicalism: Embattled and Thriving.* Chicago: The University of Chicago Press, 1998.

Spink, Kathryn. *Mother Theresa.* San Francisco: Harper, 1997.

Stafford, Tim. "Historian Ahead of His Time." *Christianity Today*, February 8, 2007. https://www.christianitytoday.com/ct/2007/february/34.87.html.

Stanley, Brian. *The Bible and the Flag: Protestant Missions and British Imperialism in the Nineteenth and Twentieth Centuries.* Leicester, UK: Apollos, 1992.

———. *The History of the Baptist Missionary Society, 1792–1992.* Edinburgh: T. & T. Clark, 1992.

———. "Founding the Centre for the Study of Christianity in the Non-Western World." In *Understanding World Christianity: The Vision and Work of Andrew F. Walls*, edited by William R. Burrows et al., 51–59. Maryknoll, NY: Orbis, 2011.

———. *A World History of Christianity in the Twentieth Century*. Princeton, NJ: Princeton University Press, 2019.

Stanton, Glenn T. "New Harvard Study Says U.S. Christianity Is Not Shrinking, but Growing Stronger." *The Federalist*, January 22, 2018. http://thefederalist.com/2018/01/22/new-harvard-research-says-u-s-christianity-not-shrinking-growing-stronger/.

Starcher, Richard L. "How Not to Collaborate with a Majority World Church." *Evangelical Missions Quarterly* 48, no. 4 (2012) 416–25.

Starling, Alan. *Seeds of Promise: World Consultation on Frontier Missions, Edinburgh '80*. Pasadena, CA: William Carey Library, 1981.

Steffan, Melissa. "The Surprising Countries Most Missionares Are Sent From and Go To." *Christianity Today*, July 25, 2013. https://www.christianitytoday.com/news/2013/july/missionaries-countries-sent-received-csgc-gordon-conwell.html.

Stetzer, Ed. "If It Doesn't Stem Its Decline, Mainline Protestantism Has Just 23 Easter Left." *The Washington Post*, April 28, 2017. http://www.pewforum.org/2012/10/09/nones-on-the-rise/.

Stone, Lyman. "'Mainline' Churches Are Emptying. The Political Effects Could Be Huge." *Vox*, July 14, 2017. https://www.vox.com/the-big-idea/2017/7/14/15959682/evangelical-mainline-voting-patterns-trump.

Strong, Josiah. *Our Country: Its Possible Future and Its Present Crisis with an introduction by Austin Phelps*. New York: Baker & Taylor for the American Home Missionary Society, 1891.

Stott, John. "Twenty Years after Lausanne: Some Personal Reflections." *International Bulletin of Missionary Research* 19, no. 2 (1995) 50–55.

Sundkler, Bengt, and Christopher Steed. *A History of the Church in Africa*. Cambridge: Cambridge University Press, 2000.

Sutton, Matthew Avery. *American Apocalypse: A History of Modern Evangelicalism*. Cambridge, MA: Harvard University Press, 2014.

Sweeny, Douglas A. *The American Evangelical Story: A History of the Movement*. Grand Rapids: Baker Academic, 2005.

Thuswaldner, Gregor. "A Converation with Peter L. Berger: 'How My Views Have Changed.'" *The Cresset: A review of literature, the arts and public affairs* 77, no. 3 (2014) 16–21.

Thiong'o, Ngũgĩ wa. *A Grain of Wheat*. New York: Penguin, 2012.

Tiedemann, R. G. "China and Its Neighbours." In *A World History of Christianity*, edited by Adrian Hastings, 369–415. Grand Rapids: Eerdmans, 1999.

Tocqueville, Alexis de. *Democracy in America*, vol. 1. Translated by Henry Reeve. New York: Langley, 1845.

Tomlinson, B. R. "What Was the Third World?" *Journal of Contemporary History* 38, no. 2 (2003) 307–21.

Treloar, Geoffrey R. *The Disruption of Evangelicalism: The Age of Torrey, Mott, McPherson and Hammond.* Downers Grove, IL: InterVarsity, 2017.

"2003 Christianity Today Book Awards." *Christianity Today* 47, no. 6. June 1, 2003.

"US Anglicans Join Kenyan Church." *BBC News*, August 30, 2017. http://news.bbc.co.uk/2/hi/africa/6970093.stm.

Van Dusen, George, to R. T. Davis. Rethy, Congo. June 1, 1951. Billy Graham Center Archives. AIM International, Collection 81. Wheaton, Illinois.

Vahanian, Gabriel. *The Death of God: The Culture of our Post-Christian Era.* New York: Braziller, 1961.

Vos, Nelvin. Review of *The Death of God*, by Gabriel Vahanian. *The Journal of Religion* 43, no. 1 (1963) 76–77.

Wacker, Grant. *America's Pastor: Billy Graham and the Shaping of a Nation.* Cambridge, MA: Harvard University Press, 2014.

Walls, Andrew F. *The Cross-Cultural Process in Christian History: Studies in the Transmission and Appropriation of Faith.* New York: Orbis, 2007.

Walls, Andrew F. "Eusebius Tries Again: Reconceiving the Study of Christian History." *International Bulletin of Missionary Research* 24, no. 3 (2000) 107–8.

Wanyoike, E. N. *An African Pastor.* Nairobi: East African Publishing House, 1974.

Wangzhi, Gao. "Y. T. Wu: A Christian Leader under Communism." In *Christianity in China: From the Eighteenth Century to the* Present, edited by Daniel Bays, 338–52. Stanford, CA: Stanford University Press, 1996.

Ward, Kevin A. *A History of Global Anglicanism.* Cambridge: Cambridge University Press, 2006.

Ward, Kevin A., and Emma Wild-Wood. *The East African Revival: Histories and Legacies.* Surrey, UK: Ashgate, 2012.

Ward, Ted. "Christian Missions—Survival in What Form?" *International Bulletin of Missionary Research* 6, no. 1 (1982) 2–3.

———. "Repositioning Mission Agencies for the Twenty-first Century." *International Bulletin of Missionary Research* 23, no. 4 (1999) 146–52.

Weber, Linda J., and Dotsey Welliver. *Mission Handbook, 2007–2009: U.S. and Canadian Ministries Overseas.* Wheaton, IL: EMIS, 2007.

"Wheaton Declaration: Subscribed by Delegates to the Congress on the Church's Worldwide Mission." Convened at Wheaton, Illinois. April 9–16, 1966. *International Review of Missions* (October 1966).

Willis, Avery T. *Indonesian Revival: Why Two Million Came to Christ.* South Pasadena, CA: William Carey Library, 1977.

Wilson, Dorothy Clarke. "Scudder, Ida Sophia." In *Biographical Dictionary of Christian Missions*, edited by Gerald H. Anderson, 609–10. New York: Macmillan, 1998.

Wilson, George Herbert. *The History of the Universities' Mission to Central Africa.* Letchworth, UK: Garden City, 1936.

Winter, Ralph. "The New Macedonia: A Revolutionary New Era in Mission Begins." In *Perspectives on the World Christian Movement*, edited by Ralph Winter and Stephen Hawthorne, 157–58. Pasadena, CA: William Carey Library, 1981.

Winter, Ralph D., and Mary Motte. "Mission in the 1990s: Two Views." *International Bulletin of Missionary Research* 14, no. 3 (1990) 100–101.

Wintle, Michael. *An Economic and Social History of the Netherlands, 1800–1920: Demographic, Economic and Social Transition*. Cambridge: Cambridge University Press, 2007.

Weber, Jeremy. "Incredible Indian Christianity: A Special Report on the World's Most Vibrant Christward Movement." *Christianity Today*, October 21, 2016. https://www.christianitytoday.com/ct/2016/november/incredible-india-christianity-special-report-christward-mov.html.

"What Is 'Back to Jerusalem'?" *Back to Jerusalem*. https://backtojerusalem.com/about/.

Wickeri, Philip L. *Reconstructing Christianity in China: K. H. Ting and the Chinese House Church*. Maryknoll, NY: Orbis, 2007.

Wiyono, Gani. "Timor Revival: A Historical Study of the Great Twentieth-Century Revival in Indonesia." *Asian Journal of Pentecostal Studies* 4, no. 2 (2001) 269–293.

Wolffe, *The Expansion of Evangelicalism: The Age of Wilberforce, More, Chalmers and Finney*. Downers Grove, IL: InterVarsity, 2007.

Woodberry, Robert D. "Reclaiming the M-Word: The Legacy of Missions in Non-Western Societies." *The Review of Faith and International Affairs* 4, no. 1 (2006) 3–12.

World Christian Database. Leiden: Brill, 2004.

Weigel, George. *Witness to Hope: The Biography of John Paul II*. London: HarperCollins, 2005.

Yale-Edinburgh Group on World Christianity and the History of Christian Mission. http://divinity-adhoc.library.yale.edu/Yale-Edinburgh/.

Young, F. Lionel III. "A 'New Breed of Missionaries': Assessing Attitudes toward Western Missions at the Nairobi Evangelical Graduate School of Theology." *International Bulletin of Missionary Research* 36, no. 2 (2012) 90–95.

Yun, Brother, Peter Xu Yongze, Enoch Wang, and Paul Hattaway. *Back to Jerusalem: Three Chinese House Church Leaders Share Their Vision to Complete the Great Commission*. Wheaton, IL: InterVarsity, 2005.

Zurlo, Gina. "David B. Barrett, 1927–2011." In *Dictionary of African Christian Biography*. Boston: Center for Global Christianity and Mission, 2017. https://dacb.org/stories/kenya/barrett-david/#.

Zurlo, Gina, et al. "World Christianity and Mission 2020: Ongoing Shift to the Global South." *International Bulletin of Missionary Research* 44, no. 1 (2019) 17.

Zwemer, Samuel M. *The Unoccupied Fields of Africa and Asia*. New York: Laymen's Missionary Movement, 1911.

Index

Aaron, Sushil J., 76n29
Achebe, Chinua, 24n60
Adam, 95
Aikman, David, 27–28, 28n77
Anderson, 55n29, 66n70, 67n72, 71n4, 72n5, 74n17
Anderson, Alan, 21n44, 84n75
Aritonang, Jan S., 27n73, 77n37, 78n43, 79n49
Arnold, David, 49n6
Athanasius of Alexandria, 23
Athyal, Jesudas M., 4n10, 26n69
Augustine of Hippo, 23
Azariah, V. S., 74–75

Bacon, Daniel W., 60n45
Bailey, Sarah Pulliam, 86n81
Barclay, Oliver, 60n46
Barnett, Erik S., 107n19
Barrett, David, 33, 36–37, 40, 41, 42–43, 44, 45, 48, 77n35, 82n65, 83, 88, 95n18, 120–21n54
Bauman, Chad M., 76n28, 76n30
Beal, David O., 20n34
Bebbington, David W., 44, 54n23
Bebbington, Eileen, 44n45
Becker, 95n21
Bediako, Kwame, 23n54, 35
Bell, James, 84n73
Belloc, Hilaire, 15
Berg, Daniel, 84
Bergen, Doris, 106n15
Berger, Peter, 31, 42
Bird, Warren, 13n5, 27n74, 74n18, 80n53
Blakeslee, Virginia, 69, 82n62
Blixen, Karen, 69
Bojaxhiu, Anjezë Gonxhe (Mother Theresa), 67
Bonhoeffer, Dietrich, 106
Bonk, Jonathan, 126n24
Borthwick, Paul, 128
Bosch, David, 8n13
Bowler, Kate, 86n82
Brainerd, David, 55–56, 58
Brereton, Virginia Lieson, 61n47
Brouwer, Steve, 86n82
Broward, Josh, 123
Brown, Callum G., 17n23
Bryan, Jack, 125n20
Budde, Michael L., 127n26
Bundy, David, 25n64
Burlin, Paul T., 67n76
Burton, Keith Augustus, 64n61

Cabrita, Joel, 40n28, 45n47
Calderón, Diego de Landa, 50
Calvin, John, 20
Cambell, Ian, 108n24
Queen Candace, 22
Carew, Douglas, 70
Carey, William, 56–57

Carpenter, Joel, 13, 43, 63n57, 97n29
Carter, Humphrey, 11n1
Cary, William, 90
Cheng-Tozun, Dorcas, 125n19
Chester, C. H., 73n11
Chestnut, R. Andrews, 85n76, 86n84
Christ, 125, 126. *See also* Jesus Christ
Church, John E. ("Joe"), 80, 81n57, 82
Coleman, Simon, 15n15
Columbus, 48, 49
Conforti, Joseph, 55n28
Connell, Raewn, 14n8
Connery, Sean, 33
Constantine, 25
Cook, James, 56
Cooperman, Alan, 19n29
Coote, Robert T., 93n13, 93n14
Corbett, Steve, 126n24, 128n28
Cross, 25n63
Cross, Frank Leslie, 33

Dados, Nour, 14n8
Daughrity, Dyron, 3–4, 26n69, 88n1
Davis, R. T., 107n19
de Gama, Vasco, 50
de Graft, Jo, 117
De Gruchy, Steve, 111n29
Dennis, James S., 42
Devitt, Edith, 65n63
Dow, Philip E., 65n63
Du Bois, W. E. B., 106, 108, 109

Eddy, Sherwood, 74–75
King Edward IV, 57n35
Edwards, Jonathan, 54, 55, 56, 58, 70
Edwards, Wendy J. Deichmann, 105n12
Endo, Shusaku, 53
Escobar, Samuel, 115n39, 128, 129n32
Esterline, David, 98n30
Evans, Richard, 9n14
Eve, 95

Farhadian, Charles E., 4–5, 17n24
Fihlani, Pumza, 97n28
Fikkert, Brian, 126n24, 128n28
Finney, Charles, 70
Francescon, Luis, 84
Pope Francis I., 21
Freston, Paul, 84n72, 85n78
Frykenberg, R. E., 25n64, 27n70, 76n31

Gatũ, John, 83, 113–14
Ghandi, Mahatma, 75
Gibson, David, 21n41
Gifford, Paul, 86n82
Githii, David Muhia, 81n59
Gonsalves, Kelly, 102n2
González, Justo I., 20n37, 20n38, 21n39, 22n45, 22n46, 50n8, 52n13, 52n15
González, Ondina E., 20n37, 20n38, 21n39, 22n45, 22n46, 50n8, 52n13, 52n15
Goodpasture, H. McKennie, 42n37
Graham, Billy, 19, 20n34, 63, 63n56, 70, 89, 106, 114
Green, Gene L., 123n10
Greenman, Jeffery P., 123n10
Groves, C. P., 24n58
Gundry, Judith, 126
Gundry, S. N., 30n91

Hardage, Jeanette, 66n71
Harder, 61n49, 62n53
Harper, Susan Billington, 74n21, 75nn22–27
Hartch, Todd, 4n9, 22n48
Hastings, Adrian, 23n56, 29n84, 35, 64n60, 64n62, 111n28

Hatch, Nathan, 19n28
Hattaway, Paul, 28n80, 28n81
Heale, Michael J., 101n1
Hendricks, Barbara, 116n46
Henman, Philip S., 112n30
Herrman, 119n53
Hertzke, 76n28
Hilliard, David, 29n84
Hitler, 106
Hollinger, David A., 107n21
Honer, Mary Anderson, 65n63
Horn, Robert M., 60n46
Howell, Brian, 128n28
Hsu, Becky, 41n34
Hughes, Hugh Price, 105
Hunt, Everett N., Jr., 72n5
Hutchinson, Mark, 13n6

Ignatius of Loyola, 53
Isaiah, 80

Jacobs, D. R., 80n55
Jacobson, Douglas, 3, 17n21, 126n26
James, 96
Jenkins, Philip, 2–3, 11, 17n23, 25n65, 25n66, 31, 47, 65n64, 84n71, 120–21, 126n26
Jenkins, Simon, 16n20
Jesus Christ, 47, 51, 96, 99
Pope John Paul II, 16
Johnson, Adelle, 124n16
Johnson, Todd M., 12n4, 14n12, 19n30, 21n43, 22n49, 24n61, 25n62, 28n78, 28n79, 29n85, 29n86, 29n87, 30n88, 30n89, 36n8, 41, 67n75, 73n16, 79n51, 79n52, 87n85, 95n18, 95n19, 124n14
Johnstone, Patrick, 22n46, 28n79, 29n86, 36n7, 99nn34–39, 100n40, 124n16
Jones, Bob, Sr., 20n34
Jones, Larry, 122
Jones, Tracy K., Jr., 115n41

Kane, J. Herbert, 114
Keen, Benjamin, 52n14
Keller, Timothy, 1
Kendi, Ibram X., 107n20
Kenyatta, Jomo, 64, 108
Keyes, Lawrence, 127
Kim, Kirsteen, 5, 72n8
Kim, Sebastian, 5, 72n8
Kings, 110n27
Kingsolver, Barbara, 46, 47, 66, 67
Kipling, Rudyard, 101, 103–4
Klingken, Gerry van, 77n40
Koch, Kurt E., 73n12, 73n15, 73n16, 79n48
Kollman, Paul V., 4n11
Kronk, Rick, 122n8
Kuzmic, Peter, 17n23
Kwong-Chan, Kim, 4n8

Lacy, Creighton, 115
Lara-Braud, Jorge, 126n23
Larsen, Timothy, 44n45
Las Casas, Bartolomé de, 52
Latourette, Kenneth Scott, 63
Lee, Timothy S., 72n6, 73n13
Lewis, C. S., 11, 37
Lewis, R. W., 93n16
Littlefield, Christina, 104n8
Livermore, David, 128n28
Livingstone, 25n63
Livingstone, David, 23, 46, 57, 58–59, 64
Lloyd, Margaret, 82n62
Lugo, Luis, 19n29
Lumumba, Patrice, 47
Luther, Martin, 16, 55
Lyall, Leslie T., 77n36
Lyon, Mary, 66

MacCulloch, Dairmaid, 50n7
Macedo, Edir, 85
MacMaster, R. K., 80n55, 81n59, 82n63
Mandryk, Jason, 22n46, 28n79, 99nn34–39, 100n40, 124n16

Mariz, Cecilia, 21n42
Marsden, George, 55n27, 56n30, 103
Marshall, Paul, 127n26
Martin, Eloísa, 21n42
Martyn, Henry, 58
Masci, David, 85n79
Massam, Katharine, 29n83
Matheson, 37n12
Mboya, Tom, 24n59
McCracken, Bret, 53n19
McGavran, Donald, 91
McIntire, Carl, 20n34
McKenzie, Robert Tracy, 105n9
Mcleod, Hugh, 29n83
McWilliams, John C., 101n1
Meredith, Martin, 24n59
Minkema, Kenneth P., 55n29
Moffett, Samuel Austin, 71–72
Moffett, Samuel Hugh, 51n9, 53n17, 53n20
Moll, Rob, 27n72
Montesinos, Antonio de, 52
Moody, D. L., 60–61, 62
Moon, Lottie, 66
Mother Theresa, 67
Mott, John R., 62, 74–75, 90
Motte, Mary, 116n44
Moyne, Samuel, 108n23
Mubulaki, Kangwa, 98n33
Muriu, Oscar, 118, 121–22
Murray, Lorraine, 22n47
Mwangi, Boniface, 118–19

Nathan Price, 46–47, 67, 103
Neely, Alan, 66n70, 71n4, 72n7
Neill, Stephen, 7, 51, 53n18, 54n21, 57n34, 88–90, 94, 96, 100
Nevius, John Livingston, 71–72
Niebuhr, Gustav, 83n70
Niebuhr, Richard, 102–3, 103n4
Njogu, Kimani, 113n34
Nkrumah, Kwame, 108
Nolde, Otto Frederick, 107–8
Noll, Mark A., 18n26, 31n96, 43–44, 44n43, 54n22, 55n24, 124n16
Nsibambi, Simeon, 80

Oden, Thomas C., 23n55
Oliver, Roland, 38
Origen of Alexandria, 23
Orr, J. Edwin, 72n9, 74n19
Ostling, 37n12

Pachua, Lalsangkima, 4
Padilla, Renè, 116
Pate, Larry, 124, 127
Apostle Paul, 15, 125
Persuad, Trevor, 70n1
Peterson, Derek R., 82n61
Phelps, Austin, 105
Pierson, A. T., 61
Piper, John, 92n11, 106
Pope Pius XII, 106
Pliny the Elder, 32
Plowman, 79n48
Pollock, John C., 60n42, 60n43, 60n44
Ponniah, James, 76n28
Porter, 110n27
Porter, Andrew, 65n66
Porterfield, Amanda, 66n69
Preston, J. Fairman, 72n10
Priest, Robert J., 123n12
Putney, Cliford, 67n76

Randall, Ian, 60n46, 67n77
Rattansi, 106n14
Reese, Robert, 114n37, 126n24
Ricci, Mateo, 53
Rice, John R., 20n34
Robert, Dana, 2, 5, 14n11, 40n27, 43, 48, 61n48, 62n50, 63n59, 65n64, 65n65, 66n68, 67n74, 68n78, 68n79, 120, 123n13, 124n14
Roberts, Gene, 102n3
Rockefeller, John D., 97

Rodin, Auguste, 103
Rose, Susan D., 86n82
Ross, Kenneth, 14n12, 21n43, 28n79, 29n86, 29n87, 30n88, 30n89
Ross, Kenneth R., 26n69

Saad, Lydia, 19n31
Sahgal, Neha, 84n73
Samuel, Vinay, 115n43
Sandgren, David P., 65n63
Sands, Kirkley, 21n43
Sankey, Ira D., 61
Sanneh, Lamin, 13, 24n60, 33, 35, 37–40, 43, 45, 48
Santoso, Aboeprijadi, 77n40
Scherer, James A., 112–13
Schuster, Kathleen, 16n18
Schwartz, Glenn, 126n24
Sciolino, Elaine, 16n16
Scott, Karen, 127n26
Scudder, Ida, 66–67
Shah, 76n28
Shaw, 98n32
Shaw, George Bernard, 10
Shaw, Mark, 14n10, 23n53, 71n2, 74n20, 84n74, 85n77
Shellnutt, Kate, 93n15
Shenk, Wibert R., 63n57
Sherwood, Harriet, 16n17, 16n19
Simeon, Charles, 57–58
Skrentny, John, 109n25
Slessor, Marry, 66
Smail, John R. W., 77n39
Smedley, Cynthia Toms, 4n11
Smith, Christian Stephen, 20n35
Spink, Kathryn, 67n73
Stafford, Tim, 33n1, 34n3
Stanley, Brian, 5, 35, 40–41, 44, 48, 57n33, 65n67, 76n32, 90n8, 106n16, 117n50
Stanley, Henry Morton, 23
Stanton, Glenn T., 20n36
Starcher, Rich, 122–23
Starling, Alan, 93n12
Steed, Christopher, 23n52, 23n57, 34n4, 51n10, 53n16
Steenbrink, Karel E., 27n73, 77n37, 78n43, 79n49
Steffan, Melissa, 95n20, 124n17
Stetzer, Ed, 19n32
Stone, Lyman, 19n33
Stott, John, 98, 114, 116, 116n45
Strong, Josiah, 105, 105n10
Studd, C. T., 60
Sugden, Chris, 115n43
Sundkler, Bengt, 23n52, 23n57, 34n4, 51n10, 53n16
Sung, John, 77
Sutton, Matthew Avery, 63n55
Sweeney, Douglas, 55

Taylor, Hudson, 61
Taylor, James Hudson, 59
Tertullian of Carthage, 23
Thiong'o, Ngũgĩ, 81n59
Apostle Thomas, 25
Tiedemann, R. G., 26n67, 51n11
Tocquevile, Alexis de, 18
Tolkien, J. R. R., 11n1
Tomlinson, B. R., 14n9
Treloar, Geoffrey R., 62n54
Turner, Harold W., 35

Vahanian, Gabriel, 30
Van Dusen, George, 107n19
Van Dusen, Henry P., 2n3
Vingren, Gunnar, 84
Volf, Miroslav, 126
Vos, Nelvin, 30n90

Wacker, Grant, 106n17
Walls, Andrew, 33–35, 38, 39, 40, 41, 45, 48, 88, 125, 126
Wang, Enoch, 28n80
Wangzhi, Gao, 27n75
Wanyoike, E. N., 81n59
Ward, Kevin A., 16n19, 81n56
Ward, Ted, 114, 115n42
Warren, Max, 110

Weber, Jeremy, 26n68
Weber, Linda J., 124n18
Weigel, George, 16n16
Welliver, Dotsey, 124n18
Wesley, John, 54
Whitefield, George, 54
Wickeri, Philip L., 27n76
Wild-Wood, Emma, 81n56
Willis, Avery T., 77n38, 78n42, 78n44, 79n47, 79n50
Willis, D., 37
Wilson, Dorothy Clarke, 67n72
Wilson, Douglas, 123n12
Wilson, George Herbert, 59n41
Winter, Ralph D., 91–93, 115–16, 116n44
Wintle, Michael, 76n34
Wiyono, 78n43
Wolffe, John, 13n6, 57n34
Woodberry, Robert D., 68n78
Wu, Y. T., 27

Xavier, Francis, 53

Yongze, Peter Xu, 28n80
Young, F. Lionel III, 117n47, 118n51
Yun, Brother, 28n80

Zurlo, Gina, 12n4, 19n30, 21n40, 22n49, 24n61, 25n62, 28n78, 28n82, 29n85, 36n9, 37n11, 42, 63n58, 67n75, 73n16, 79n51, 79n52, 87n85, 95n19, 124n16
Zwemer, Samuel M., 90

Made in the USA
Columbia, SC
19 August 2024